CW01651076

Walks

Published in 1996 by

The Moor, Dale and Mountain Press,
South Down,
Bratton Fleming,
Barnstaple,
Devon. U.K.
EX31 4TQ.

ISBN 1 899183 29 9

The Moor, Dale and Mountain Press

Bratton Fleming

IMPORTANT NOTE. Whilst every effort has been made by the author to determine the most appropriate and correct routes whilst actually walking the paths no responsibility whatsoever can be accepted by the author or the publisher for precision at time of use by the purchaser or by anyone. Occasionally a path that is frequently used by the public and that is not necessarily a public right of way has been included within this series. Anyone using any part of the routes described in this publication does so entirely at their own discretion.

All of the heights above sea level and grid references stated in this publication are approximate and are derived from the O.S. Landranger maps for the area which are Landranger 180 and 181.

Exmoor
The Walks

continued

How to use the guide

This part of the page shows how the walk can be found on a road map or from road signs.

The text thoroughly describes the route and each walk has been selected to include the most contrasting range of natural scenery.

All the walks are circular walks and can be started at any point. The figures before the brackets at the start of paragraphs are the locations on the sketch.

If it is probable that the walk is impassable in winter a note is included in the text of any available alternatives. When referring to rivers and riverbanks the text sometimes refers to "downstream near the left bank" which does mean the left side of the river when looking downstream and "upstream near the left bank" which does mean the left side of the river when looking upstream.

Grid references are shown in brackets for walkers who like to use maps.

Sample Page and Explanatory Notes.

On the A361, South Molton to Bampton, turn left about 9km (5 miles) from S. Molton on to a minor road signed to Molland. Continue past the Molland Church for about 250m to where the road bends left. Turn off here to continue directly on for about 400m and then turn left on to the no through lane for about 750m to just before where the tarmac lane bends sharp right. It should be possible to park off the road here, on the left.

1.(814290) Our route goes back to the junction, turns left over a stile to go across the top of three fields with a bank on the left and then continues down across the next field to a stile on to a lane. On the lane our route turns left for about 250m to the first sharp right bend at 2.

2.(819282) Here our route leaves the lane to continue directly on along a track to Whitley Farm where our route follows the track through a field gate, past the house on the left and to another field gate at 3.

3.(827281) Through this field gate our route turns left on the track down into the valley and continues near the left bank of the stream to a field gate where there is a small ford on the right. Our route goes over the ford and through a field gate to continue between the wood and the stream for about 200m to join another path. Here our route continues slightly to the left and gradually climbs out of the valley on a path between two banks to Brimblecombe at 4.

4.(831288) At Brimblecombe our route joins a track and keeps to the left of the buildings to go through a field gate and continue up a track which bears left after

6km (4 miles).
The scenery is very good. The route includes rolling farmland, a river valley and moorland.
Can be muddy in winter.
Some modest slopes.
Overall from 190 metres up to 330 metres.
There is no public transport to this walk.
Parking is possible at 1.
There is a pub at Molland and tearooms at Exford and South Molton.

This part of the page provides an overview of the walk and the facilities.

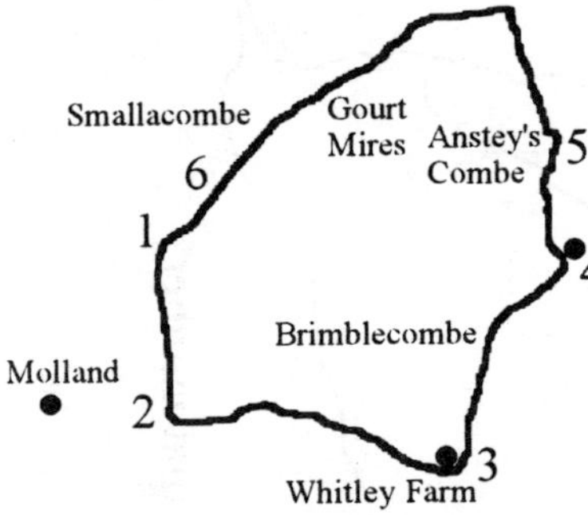

There should be sufficient space on the sketch maps to mark any locations of your own.
All the sketch maps share the same approximate scale which is 2cm per kilometre or 3.2cm per mile.
The orientation of all sketch maps is that approximate grid north is towards the top of the page.
On coastal walks the heavier black line is an indication of the mean tide mark, not the cliff edge.

about 200m to go across the fields and on to the moorland at 5.

5.(830293) *If the visibility is poor it may be preferable to turn left on to the bridleway that runs along the edge of the moorland for about 1.5km to 6.* Our route continues up and slightly to the right, on to the moor and as far as where the first broad bridleway bears off to the left. Here our route bears off to the left to continue slightly uphill along the right hand side of a combe and then bears left across the top of the combe. Then our route continues across the top of a smaller combe to join another track on which our route turns left. Our route follows this track above a combe that progressively deepens on the right to near the edge of the moor where the track goes down in to the combe to cross a shallow ford, to go over a small bridge and to reach a field gate at the edge of the moor at 6.

6.(816291) Here our route goes through the field gate and on to a lane back to 1.

Over moors, heaths and mountains it is frequently useful at some times of the year to carry a compass and on the walks to which this applies approximate compass directions are included in brackets. All distances stated are approximate.

The word "lane" is used to describe a road on which two vehicles could not usually pass and the word "track" is used when the condition of the surface makes it unlikely to be used by most cars.

Exmoor area

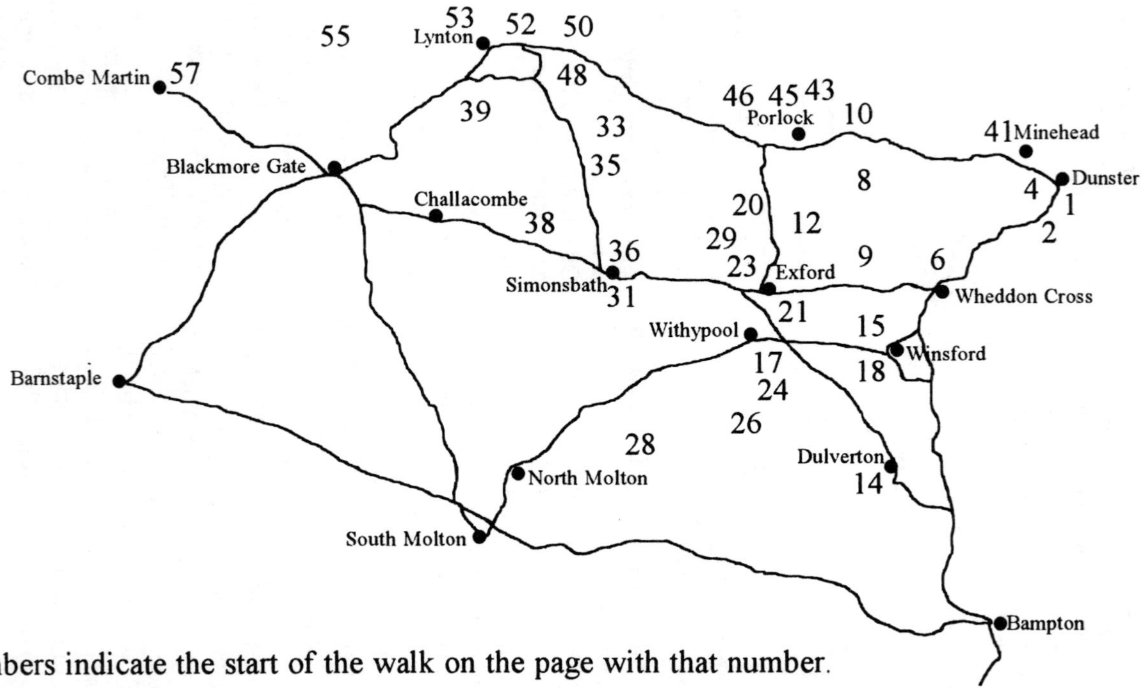

The numbers indicate the start of the walk on the page with that number.

The lines indicate frequently used roads.

Dunster, Vinegar Hill and Bat's Castle.

Entering Dunster on the A396 from Wheddon Cross there is a car park near the end of Park Street which is on the right next to The Foresters Arms. This walk starts from the car park which is at 1 in the notes.

5km (3 miles).
The scenery is good.
A walk through mature mixed woodland, over heath and through ancient and mixed woodland.
There are some good views over the Severn Estuary, over Dunster, inland over woodland and towards the heath of Dunkery Beacon.
Usually good walking all year round.
Overall from 30 metres up to 210 metres.
Some modest slopes.
Dunster is on a regular bus route.
There is a car park at 1.
There are tearooms and pubs in Dunster.

1.(990433) From the car park our route turns left, down the lane and over the bridge and continues to the left of the thatched cottages. Just past the thatched cottages there is a junction of paths and our route follows the second from the right signed Timberscombe via Croydon Hill. With the exception of the path to the left that is gated and is about 400m from the cottages our route keeps to the left at any forks or junctions for about 1km from the thatched cottages, to 2.

2.(982426) Here our route turns on to the first obvious path on the left that doubles back on our route to curve up through the wood to a pair of stiles. Our route goes over both the stiles and then keeps to the left to follow the path that curves up and to the right to become a broader path along the top of the hill. This broad path continues along the top of the hill to go over some ancient forts and into a coniferous forest where it ends at some field gates at 3.

3.(993419) Immediately before the field gates our route turns left on a bridleway to Dunster. When the track first forks, about 300m from the gates, to become two obvious tracks our route keeps to the left and just over 500m further on when the track forks again our route keeps to the right to curve down through some mixed, and then some very old woods Near the bottom of the wood there is a pair of gates across our route. Our route continues through these and on for a few metres to join another path. Here our route turns left to go over a stile and then turns right to pass in front of the thatched cottages and back to the car park.

Broadwood, Withycombe Common and Clicket.

Following the A396 from Dunster to Wheddon Cross turn left approx. 1km from Dunster on to a minor road. About 1km on the left is the Crown Estates car park at 1.

13 km (8 miles).
The scenery is good. Primarily a woodland walk partly through mixed forest, over heath and then through deciduous woods above a brook.
There are a few good views, mainly from the top of Withycombe Common, over the Severn Estuary, inland over woodland and towards the heath of Dunkery Beacon.
A rugged path in parts and can be wet in winter. Usually good walking from summer through to late autumn. Very much away from the crowds.
Overall from 90 metres up to 381 metres.
Some modest slopes.
There is no public transport to this walk.
There is a car park at 1.
The nearest tearooms and pubs are at Dunster.
The Crown Estates have some trails marked from the same starting point and these are generally over less wet and more frequented paths.

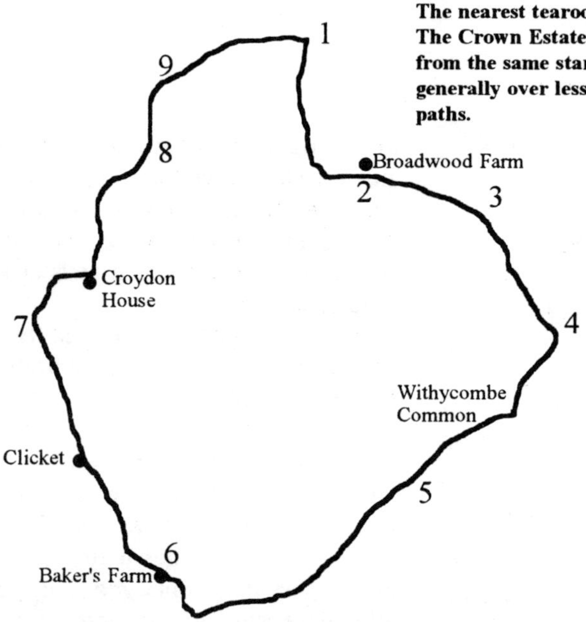

1.(977423) From the Crown Estates car park our route follows the main track up through the picnic area and continues to where another track comes down from the right to join our route just where it begins to level off. Here our route turns left on a bridleway that has the remains of an old stone bank on the left and then goes down and across some boards over a wet area and then continues, just inside the wood and with the fields to the left, to a track at 2.

2.(979414) Here our route turns right on the track and then right again on the next track which has a tarmac surface and continues past Broadwood Farm for about 100m to a field gate on the right where the track bears left. Our route goes through the field gate and follows a footpath around the left side of the field, close to the hedge, over a bridge and then continues along the left side of the next field to a gate on to a track. Our route follows this track down through a wood on a deteriorating path to some stepping stones over a brook at 3.

3.(987412) Just after the brook our route takes the third turning off on the left to go up through the wood on a path and then turns right on a track at a T-junction. Our route goes up this track for about 1km to where the heath begins on the right at 4.

4.(993402) Our route continues on up the track, with heath on the right, for about 800m, to just after where the trees have been cleared on the left, and then follows the track as it curves up and to the right to pass the triangulation point near the top of Withycombe Common and then continues to a junction of 6 tracks at 5.

5.(984394) From this junction our route goes directly on with deciduous trees on the left and conifers on the right, to the bottom of the track. Here our route turns right on the lane for about 300m to the second right hand bend where Baker's Farm is on the left at 6.

6.(968387) Our route leaves the lane at this sharp bend and continues directly on through a gate and along a track with banks on either side to a stile on the right. Over this stile our route goes across a field into a wood and keeps to the right on a path that is fairly obvious to the first brook that crosses this path. Here our route follows the bed of the brook to an old stone bridge and then continues down the left side of the stream to a wooden footbridge where the path forks at 7.

7.(959405) Our route goes over the footbridge and across the field on a track that curves to the left and up the other side of the valley to a field gate. Just through this gate our route turns left through a gate marked "Path avoiding mud" and then turns immediately right along the top of the fields to some steps leading up to a track. Our route turns left on this track and then takes the right fork up a track to the edge of the coniferous wood to a gate across the track. Our route goes through this gate into the field and keeps to the right when the track forks and continues to curve gradually up, to the right and to the top of the field near 8.

8.(967416) Here the correct path appears to be rather vague and the simplest solution is probably to follow the track through the field gate and on to the forestry land where our route turns left. There should be a bridleway going across the heath but this is also rather vague so the simplest solution is probably to continue down the track for about .5km to where the track bears right and then a bridleway joins from the left at the edge of a wood at 9.

9.(967420) Again, the correct path is a little vague so our route continues to where the track forks. Here our route forks left and on the left side of the track is a stone wall. Our route continues on the left side of the stone wall to a T-junction where our route turns right for about 10m and then left down a bridleway through a wood to where the area on the right has been cleared. Our route continues directly on to where this track bears sharp left and a less used track turns off to the right, here our route turns off to the right to the lane. On the lane our route turns left to the car park on the right at 1.

Dunster, Alcombe Common, Wootton Common and Hopcott Common.

10km (6 miles).
The scenery is pleasant
A walk through mature oak woodlands, over open heath and through coniferous woods. There are some good views over the Severn Estuary and inland over pastoral scenes and towards the heath of Dunkery Beacon.
Usually good walking all year round.
Overall from 50 metres up to 295 metres.
Some modest slopes.
Dunster is on a regular bus route.
Parking is possible near 1 and 5.
There are tearooms and pubs in Dunster.

Entering Dunster on the A396 from Wheddon Cross there is a car park near the end of Park Street which is on the right immediately before The Foresters Arms. Further along the A396, just before the traffic lights, St. George's Street is on the left and up this street there is a lane on the left, just past the school. This is point 1 in the notes.
Alternatively there is a minor road called Periton Lane which is virtually the southern boundary of the Minehead built up area. Periton Lane joins, at both ends, the A39. From Dunster, there is a lane off Periton Lane on the left called Hopcott. At the top of this lane there is a place for parking and it is within a few metres of 5. Walking directly on up from the Hopcott parking space there is a track which is joined from the right by a path opposite which there is a field gate on the left. This is point 5 in the notes.

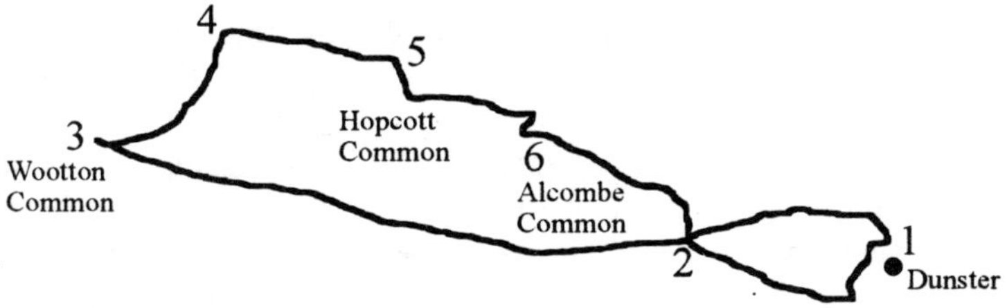

1.(990437) Our route follows the lane off St. George's Street along the side of the school and then turns left on the path around the back of the school and continues to a gate to the right of an entrance to a cemetery. Through the gate our route continues past a path immediately on the right and past the two paths on the left to curve progressively up through the oak wood for about 1km to 2.
2.(979437) Here, at the top of the wood, four paths meet and our route turns left, on a broad path more or less along the brow of the hill for about 3km. On the way, when the path forks with a field gate in the centre of the fork, our route takes the right hand path to continue with the remains of a stone bank on the left of the path. Our route continues to a triangulation pillar, hidden in the trees on the bank on the left, at 3, which is about 3km from the oak wood at 2.

3.(948442) From the triangulation pillar our route returns on the broad path for about 80m and continues down the first path on the left for about 1km, going past two paths on the left, to a path on the right signed "Griffs Path Hopcott 1 mile" at 4.
4.(955448) Our route turns right on this path which continues along the lower edge of the wood. At the end of this path our route turns right, at 5, just a few metres before a field gate.
5.(964446) Our route goes up a good path with the field edge on the left and bears around to the left to continue near the field edge but at the end of the field, just under 500m from 5, where a path turns off to the left to continue around the field and up a small hill, our route continues on down to a stream and on the way down keeps to the obvious path by bearing sharp right at the hairpin bend. At the stream our route turns left for a few metres to a ford at 6.
6.(971442) Here our route goes across the stream and takes the most right hand of the three tracks to continue between the field and the wood for just a few metres to the first bridleway going up into the wood on the left. Our route goes past some small paths on the left and then continues almost directly on along a good path signed to Dunster from a junction where another bridleway turns off to the left. From here our route goes across some heath then upwards and bears to the right to pass near the side of a field on the left to return to 2. From here there is a choice of either returning down through the shelter of the oak wood or turning left on the bridleway that goes through the edge of the wood near the field. This route keeps to the left when the path forks and arrives at a junction where our route turns right through a gate just past a small field on the right. From the gate our route continues down between two hedges to St. George's Street in Dunster and turns right, down to 1.

Exmoor is an unusual, if not unique, mix of heath, deep river valleys, moorland, shallow brooks, dramatic cliffs, small harbours, natural woodland, farming and much more.
When defining the walks to be included in this booklet as much emphasis as possible was put on two points. The first was to avoid the inclusion of roads and lanes from which the scene could easily be observed by many cars. The second was to include within each walk as much variation of type of scenery as possible.

Blagdon Wood, Dunkery Errish and Hanny Combe.

On the B3224 from Wheddon Cross to Exford there is a sharp left bend about 1km from Wheddon Cross and on the right at this bend there is a very minor lane signed Drapers Way and Steart. Just over 1.5km (1 mile) down this lane on the left is the drive up to West Harwood farm and past this drive it is possible to park on the right, at 1, and further down the lane it is also possible to park on the left.

10km (6 miles).
The scenery is very good.
A walk through rolling farmland, through deciduous and coniferous woodland, and over moorland.
Some pleasant views over rolling moorland and rural scenery.
Part of this walk is over a rugged path and can be very wet in winter.
Away from the crowds.
Overall from 137 metres up to 332 metres.
Some modest slopes.
There is no public transport to this walk but the regular bus service along the A396 passes about .5km from point 7.
Car parking is possible near 1.
There is a tearoom and a pub at Wheddon Cross.

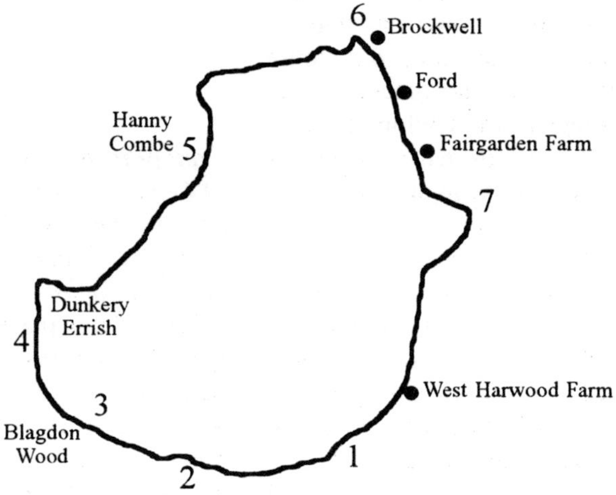

1.(932400) Our route goes back up the lane, past the track to West Harwood Farm on the right, past the track to North Hawkwell on the right, over the bridge and past the track on the right to Walland Farm and on for about another 125m to a field gate on the right at 2.

2.(919399) From this field gate our route follows a bridleway on a track that goes down the edge of the field, over a bridge and through a gate at the edge of the wood. Our route continues on the track near the edge of the wood, with a brook down on the right, for about 300m to cross a ford just after a derelict stone wall on the right at 3.

3.(912401) Our route goes up the right side of the brook on the track to the next ford and then continues up the left side of the brook for about 300m to where the bridleway forks. This point can be easy to miss. Here our route leaves the track which bears to the left. Our route, which is very little used, fords the brook and then continues up the left side of a smaller brook to cross a track. Our route continues near the right hand side of a derelict stone bank for a few metres and then bears right, up through the bracken on a path to a field gate at 4.

4.(910407) Through the field gate there are numerous paths, most of which are animal tracks, that go up through the bracken. Over on the right there are some beech trees on top of a field boundary bank and our route goes up through the bracken, near the left side of the bank, and joins a track near the top corner of that field boundary bank. Our route turns right on this track to continue on the edge of the moorland side of the beech trees that are along the top of the fields, to where the beech trees have been cut to make a beech hedge on the bank. When the hedge ends and the trees start again our route continues for about 50m to where the paths fork. Here our route continues straight on to follow a track that moves away from the beech trees and across the moor for about 1km to 5.

5.(919417) Here our route follows the track down through Hanny Combe, across the small brook that runs through the combe, and up the other side to continue near the edge of the heath to where the track is very near the top corner of the fields. Our route turns right at this point to continue on the track that goes gradually down the heath side of the bank between the fields and the heath to a tarmac lane at 6.

6.(929428) Here our route turns right on the tarmac lane for about 1,300m to pass Brockwell which is on the left, to pass through Ford, to pass Fairgarden Farm which is also on the left and when the tarmac lane bears sharp right our route continues directly on along a track between two hedges. The track goes down and over a ford and then continues for about 250m to where the first track turns off to the right at 7.

7.(938416) Our route follows this track to the right to where there are double field gates. Our route goes through these to continue past a barn on the left and, keeping to the left side of the field, goes through a gap in the derelict hedge bank at the far end of the field and into the next field. Here our route continues along the left side of the field to go through the gate near the corner and then directly across the next field to go through the gate in the lower corner on the far side. Through this gate our route keeps to the left side of the field to continue directly on to a track past West Harwood Farm on the left. Past the farm our route continues down the tarmac farm drive on to the tarmac lane where our route turns left back to 1.

Horner, Horner Water, and Webber's Post.

From Porlock follow the A39 towards Minehead for about 1km to a minor road on the right signed to West Luccombe and Horner. About 1km along this minor road there is an Exmoor Park car park on the left at Horner at 1.

1.(898455) From the car park entrance our route turns left on the road to the left bend and then turns right on a track that goes over a bridge and then bends left to continue up the right side of Horner Water for about 1.5km to turn left on a footbridge over the river at 2.
2.(897441) Over the footbridge our route continues directly on a path to a river and continues up the right bank to a footbridge. Over the footbridge our route turns right to continue up the left bank of the river for about 300m to the first bridleway that goes up on the left. Our route goes up this bridleway to join another path near the edge of a conifer plantation where our route turns right to the car park at Webber's Post. Our route goes across the car park to the lane and then directly across a few metres of moorland to another lane on which our route turns right for about 250m to the second bridleway on the left, at 3, which goes across open heath and is signed from the edge of the lane. (The first bridleway is not so clearly signed and goes off to the left along the edge of the wood.)
3.(903437) Our route follows the second bridleway for about 1.5km to then turn off, left, down the first bridleway that goes into a small wood and turns left on a good path that runs along the edge of the wood, past the Woodcock Gardens

8km (5 mile).
The scenery is very good.
A walk through wooded river valleys, across moorland and through deciduous and coniferous woodland.
There are some very good views over rolling moorland and rural scenery.
Usually good walking all year round but can be muddy in a few places in winter.
Overall from 65 metres up to 258 metres.
Some modest slopes and a steep one.
Horner is on a regular bus route.
There is a car park at 1 and another near 3.
There is a tearoom at Horner and there are pubs and tearooms in Porlock.

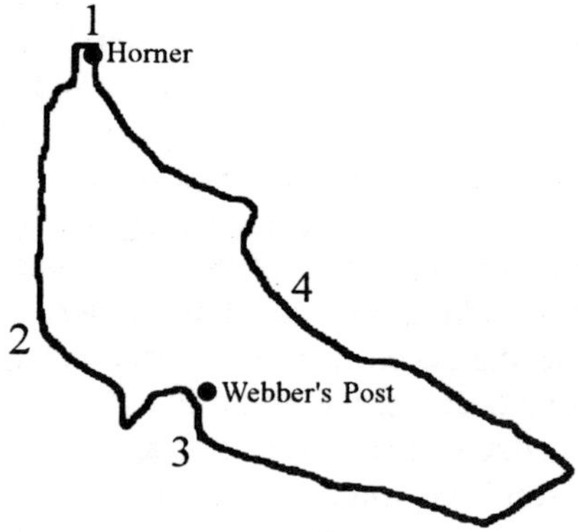

Nature Reserve, then past some open moorland to a deer gate. Through this gate our route continues directly on, on a good path usually near the edge of the wood, for just under 1km to where another path goes across our route at 4.
4.(909442) Our route continues directly on for about 750m to a lane on which our route turns right and then immediately left on to another lane at the crossroads. Our route goes past the disused quarry on the left and then goes through the field gate on the left on a track that is along the edge of the wood for just under 1km to where it comes down on to a lane and turns left. Just past the mill and just before the tearoom on the right a path turns off on the right, back to the car park.

Dunkery Bridge, Dunkery Errish and Dunkery Beacon.

Travelling south from Dunster on the A396 turn right at Wheddon Cross on to the B3224 for about 1km to where this road curves to the left and there are two lanes off to the right. Take the second lane, which continues almost straight on, for about 2.5km to Dunkery Gate which is where the lane goes over a cattle grid and on to the moorland. There is a parking area almost immediately on the right at 1.

1.(895406) From the parking area our route follows a bridleway away from the road and Dunkery Beacon on a track that goes through a field gate and continues for about 900m to ford a small stream and to continue into what was once a field with a hedge bank. From here our route follows a track gradually down to the right and then goes abruptly down to the right to a small gate at 2 which is about 150m downstream from the ford.

2.(904406) Through the gate our route turns left and continues along the top of some old fields to where there are two gaps in a bank and from the one on the right, which has paint on an overhanging bough, a track progressively leads down into the valley to where there is a stream on the left at 3.

3.(909405) Our route continues on the track for about 50m and then turns left, across the stream on to a little used path. This path goes up the left bank of a smaller brook to cross a track and to continue up a path between two banks. When the banks open out our route continues up and to the right to reach a

6km (4 miles).
The scenery is the very best.
The walk is through some woodland and pastoral farmland to a river valley and over open moorland.
Usually good walking all year round but might be difficult after very heavy rains in winter.
Some modest slopes.
Overall from 220 metres up to 515 metres.
There is no public transport to this walk.
There is a car park at 1.
There is a tearoom and a pub at Wheddon Cross and a tearoom at Horner.

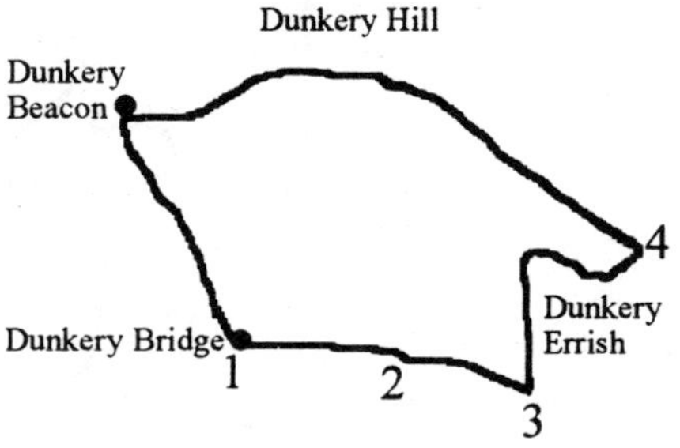

field gate. Through the field gate our route continues along the bracken side of some trees that are on a bank. At the top corner of the trees our route follows the field bank around to the right for about 250m to cross a track that goes into the field. About 200m further on a track turns off to the left to go up towards Dunkery Beacon from a fingerpost at 4. (If the visibility is bad keep to the hedge side for this 200m to a field gate where the moorland juts down towards the fields and then turn left to go up the track.)

4.(914410) Here our route follows the track up towards Dunkery Beacon and comes to a lane. If the visibility is bad it is preferable to turn left on the lane to the car park at 1. Our route goes directly across the lane to join another track and to continue up to Dunkery. From the top a path on the left goes down to 1.

Bury Castle, Selworthy Beacon and Bossington Hill.

Travelling towards Porlock on the A39 from Minehead turn right about 6km (4 miles) from Minehead on to a minor road signed to Selworthy. There is a car park in Selworthy near the church at 1.

5km (3 miles).
The scenery is the very best. The walk is over some of the best viewpoints of Exmoor and includes some of the most scenic and contrasting views of coast and countryside.
Good walking all year round.
Some steep slopes.
Overall from 50 metres up to 308 metres.
There is no public transport to this walk but Allerford is about .5km from this walk and is on a regular bus route.
There is a car park at 1.
There are tearooms at Selworthy, Allerford and Bossington and pubs and tearooms at Porlock.

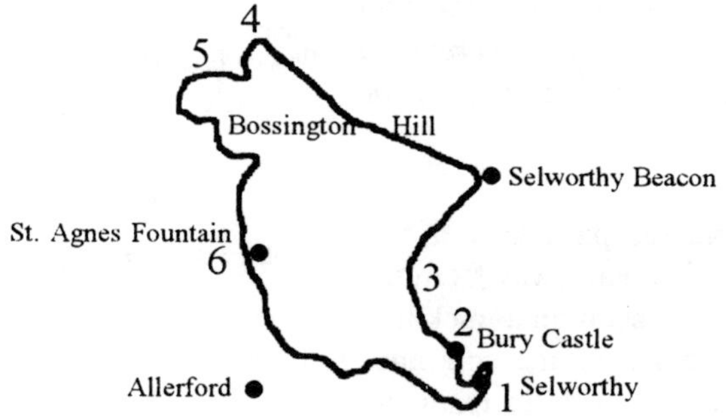

1.(920468) From the car park our route goes back down the lane, around the side of the churchyard and through a field gate to continue around the west side of the church on a track. Our route leaves the track on the first path down to the left, goes over a footbridge and keeps to the left to go through a field gate. Through the gate our route keeps to the right at the first fork and then takes the next path off on the right to Bury Castle and continues up this path, bends to the left to go past a stile that is on the right and continues on to join a wider path on which our route turns right. At the first sharp left bend our route turns off to the right on a smaller path that immediately turns left and goes up the hill, over a stile and continues to join a grass path at 2.

2.(918471) Here our route turns left and follows this path as it curves around to the right to the highest part of Bury Castle where our route turns left on a wide path across an open area and, in the silver birch wood, forks to the right to pass the Memorial Hut at 3.

3.(915477) Here our route goes across the lane and follows the track that goes up and to the right to Selworthy Beacon where our route turns left on to another track that goes down near to the corner of the fields where it continues directly on along a track which is also the Coast Path. When this track forks, with one track going off to the left to Lynch, our route continues to the right and when it forks again with a path going off and slightly up to the right our route goes to the left to remain on the Coast Path to where five paths almost meet and the Coast Path begins to go down into Hurlstone Combe at 4.

4.(904488) Our route takes the first path on the left before Hurlstone Combe, the path that doubles back slightly, and follows this path to join another good path on which it turns right to the cairn on Bossington Hill at 5.

5.(903485) Our route follows a small path past the left side of the cairn and down over the hill to join a very good path on which our route turns left. *The path down from the cairn is exceptionally steep and can be avoided by retracing the path from the cairn to 4 and then taking the next turning to the left that goes around the top of Hurlstone Combe.* Our route follows this path to cross a track and to continue through the small gate and on to where six paths meet where there is a small spring on the left called St. Agnes Fountain at 6.

6.(905474) Our route keeps to the left and continues, without turning off to the left or right when other paths cross, for about 1.5km to where a track can be seen to go down to the buildings at Selworthy on the right at a fork. Here our route keeps to the left to come down to a stile. Our route turns right over the stile into Selworthy Green and keeps to the left to go up to the car park, at 1.

From the entrance to Selworthy Church the view over Porlock Vale is excellent and some people find the half dozen or so thatched cottages around Selworthy Green to be a pleasant part of the view.

Fortunately there are not many other buildings on this walk. There are the silent remains of Bury Castle, an Iron Age enclosure, sitting on the hill overlooking the hamlet. The outer ditch encloses about one and a half hectares and the inner ditch encloses about half a hectare, the remains of part of a community. Further along our path there is a hut that was erected in memory of an owner of this estate by a member of his family who migrated to another very scenically beautiful part of the world.

For the rest of this walk there are only glimpses of buildings. For much of the route the walk is over heath which for much of the year is ablaze with the colours of heather and the late flowering western gorse and there are panoramic views across Porlock Bay, Porlock Weir and on to the wooded cliffs of Glenthorne and to Foreland Point.

From around Selworthy Beacon and Bossington Hill the inland scene extends to the large hill that is Dunkery Beacon. On the way back to Selworthy our path is near the edge of the wood and at all times of the year the view through the trees and the occasional clearings, across the valley towards Horner and Dunkery is a pastoral scene of exceptional quality.

Stoke Pero Common, East Water Valley and Dunkery Beacon.

Entering Exford on the B3224 from Wheddon Cross there is a minor road on the right that is signed to Porlock. Follow this minor road for about 2km to just over a cattle grid and then turn right on to a lane and continue for about 2.5km to a National Trust car park on the right where the road curves down to the left at 1.

12km (8 miles).
The scenery is the very best. The walk is through river valleys and over open moorland and heath.
The first 4km of this walk are over tracks and paths that are not maintained and include a large number of what are usually shallow fords but in winter after heavy rain a certain amount of agility is required to avoid wet feet.
Some modest slopes and a steep one.
Overall from 90 metres up to 519 metres.
There is no public transport to this walk.
There is a car park at 1.
There is a tearoom at Horner and pubs and tearooms at Exford and Porlock.

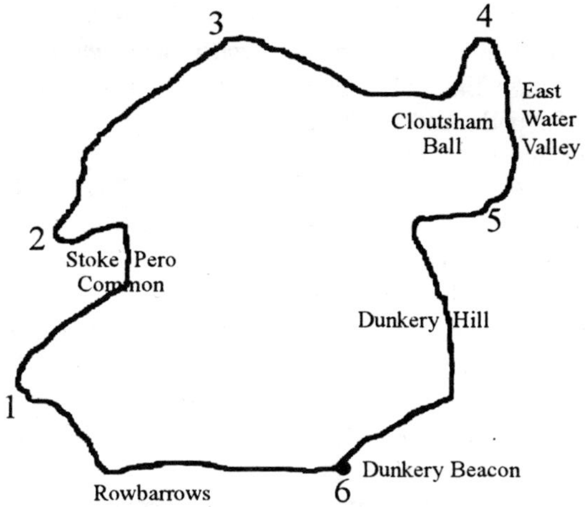

1.(871419) From the car park our route goes across the lane on to the moorland and turns right to follow a path that is more or less parallel with the lane for about 1km to where the path comes fairly close to a lane. Here our route joins a path that goes off to the left and continues to the left end of the row of pine trees and then joins an obvious path that doubles back, down across the moor and into the valley at 2.

2.(872428) When this path reaches the small trees our route turns off to the right on a smaller path that goes down to the right bank of the river and continues down either side of the river for almost 2km. On the way down our route goes across a lane after which it continues down the right bank and then there are many fords.

3.(883441) Here our route goes over a footbridge that is over a river that comes in from the left. Our route then turns right to continue down the left bank of the river for just over 1km to go over a footbridge that is a few metres on the right after the track forks, at 4, and where there is another valley on the right.

4.(897440) Over the footbridge our route continues up the valley on a good path to come to another river on the left and to go over a footbridge. Our route continues up the left bank of the river but crosses a number of footbridges to remain on the path that is always fairly near either of the riverbanks for about 1km to where it joins a lane at 5.

5.(898430) Our route continues up river, on the lane, for about half a kilometre to go over the next footbridge on the left to cross the river. (If the clouds have come down on to Dunkery and if it is preferred to avoid the heath and the moorland paths to the top it is possible to return to the car park at 1 by continuing on this lane for about 2.5km). Our route then continues on a path that goes up the hillside and curves to the left to go up through the wood and continues on to the heath. For about 1km our route continues to climb on the same obvious path that continues over the heath to the top of the combe on the right where it bears right around the top of the combe and then continues up to Dunkery Beacon at 6.

6.(892416) From Dunkery Beacon our route follows the track, west, towards the pile of stones on the next hilltop. Passing to the left of this heap of stones our route continues on to the next heap of stones and curves to the right as it goes past it to continue to the car park at 1.

An open area of heath and moorland and a distant row of pine trees: nearing the trees the view to the right is over the broad heather clad slopes of Dunkery Hill and as the path turns away from the row of trees the scene is the surrounding slopes.

As the path nears the valley the sound of the brook rises through the trees.

Down through the valley the brook is joined by more as the valley widens and is filled with old deciduous trees, birdsong and dappled light and now the stream flows over boulders and rocks that it has rounded and smoothed like the curve where another wooded valley joins. The path goes up this valley, crossing the brook a few times on footbridges to eventually leave the old trees and to come on to open heath and moorland and to climb to Dunkery Beacon.

From here some will enjoy the views north over the wooded valleys, some will enjoy the views to the east over the heather slopes and some will time their arrival for late evening when the colours of the hills to the west and south blend with the shadows of the valleys.

The path from Dunkery Beacon is towards the west and at dusk the outlines assume a positiveness that contrasts well with the orange and gold of sunset.

Dulverton, River Barle, Hinam and Chilcott.

Entering Dulverton on the B3222 from the south there is a car park on the left at 1 which is immediately after the road bridge over the River Barle.

10km (6 miles).
The scenery is very good.
A walk through riverside woodland and over rolling farmland.
Usually good walking all year round.
Overall from 150 metres up to 264 metres.
Some modest slopes.
Dulverton is on a regular bus route.
There is a car park at 1.
There are tearooms and pubs in Dulverton.

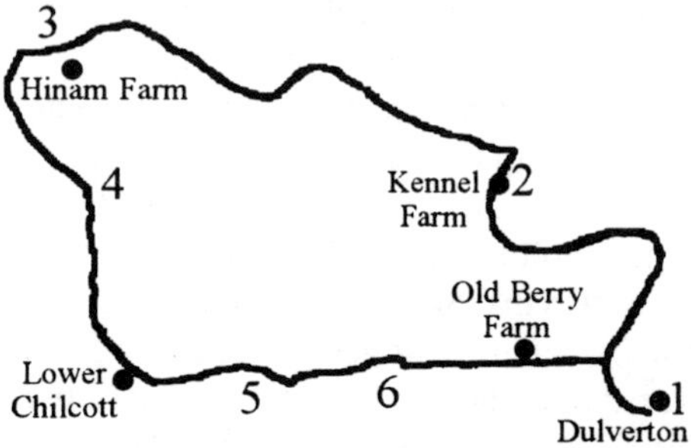

1.(912279) From the car park our route returns to the road and turns right over the bridge and then right to follow the lane up to take the right fork, uphill, with Rose Cottage on the left, and to continue to Horner Cottage where the path forks again to Tarr Steps or Beech Tree. Our route takes the right track towards Tarr Steps and when the track nears the fields at the bottom of the wood our route follows it round to the left to, and through, Kennel Farm after which our route turns right on the lane at 2.

2.(905287) Our route continues to just past the first cottage on the left and here it turns left to follow the track that is signed to Tarr Steps for just over 2km to where a smaller path leaves the track to go down on the right at 3.

3.(884292) Here our route continues on the track, up and around to the left, to a lane on which it turns right for about .5km to a small field gate on the right at 4.

4.(887287) Our route goes through this gate, up the left side of the field, through/over the field gate at the top and on to a lane to continue to Lower Chilcott on another lane that is almost directly opposite. At Lower Chilcott the tarmac ends and our route then goes through the first field gate on the left and diagonally to the right across the field to go through another small gate into a field and then immediately left again through a field gate and into a field at 5.

5.(892279) From here our route goes down and to the right on a vague track to cross the brook about half way down the field and to continue down the valley but gradually rising above the brook to a small field gate in a corner of the field about 120m above the brook. Through this gate our route goes up the valley to the right and past the two oak trees to go through a field gate at the top and on to a lane. Our route turns right on the lane to a stile on the left at 6 which is a few metres past the first track.

6.(902280) Our route goes over this stile and across the field keeping slightly to the right and then continues along the top of the field to go through a small gate in the top far corner. Then our route goes across the field to another small gate just to the right of the farm buildings and continues across the lane, through a field gate and directly across the left side of the field. About 20m before the corner of the field our route goes through a field gate and down the track to Horner Cottage where it turns right on the track back to Dulverton.

Winsford, Withycombe, The Punchbowl and Yellowcombe.

Travelling south from Wheddon Cross for about 5km (3 miles) on the A396 turn right on to a minor road signed Winsford. There is a car park in Winsford, at 1, adjacent to the tearooms.

8km (5 miles). A compass can be useful if the cloud is low because the top is a little featureless and can be confusing.
The scenery is very good.
A walk through rolling farmland, over moorland and through a small area of deciduous and coniferous woodland.
Usually good walking all year round although slightly muddy at Yellowcombe during winter.
Overall from 200 metres up to 408 metres.
Some modest slopes.
On certain days of the week there is a bus service to Winsford.
There is a car park at 1.
There is a tearoom and a pub at Winsford.

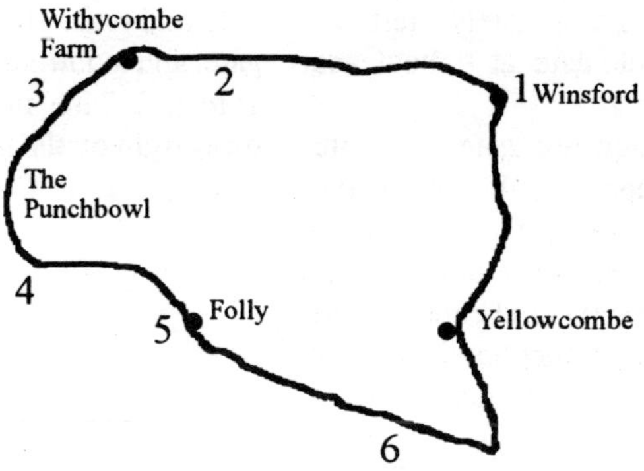

1.(906350) From the car park our route goes around the front of the tearooms, over the footbridge by the side of the ford and continues up Ash Lane, past the church on the right hand side, for about .5km to where the road bends slightly to the right and a footpath is signed to the left over a track towards two fields gates. Our route follows this footpath and turns right over a stile just before the field gates and then follows a well signed path over stiles to a small field gate. From this gate our route goes across the field on an obvious old track to another gate from where our route continues across another field to the upper of the two field gates in the opposite hedge. Through this gate our route goes across the lower side of the field to go through a small gate and continue across the next field to a field gate at 2.

2.(891351) Through this gate our route goes across the bottom of the field, above the ruined barn, to go through another field gate and across another field towards two field gates in the opposite hedge. On maps the right of way is shown as going through the lower gate and then between the farm buildings but the waymarks indicate that the path goes through the upper gate and across the bottom of the next field to join a bridleway that comes down the hill from the right on a track and this is probably the better path. The choice is yours. Our route turns left on the bridleway to cross the bridge over the brook at Withycombe Farm and continues on the track as it bends up and to the right, to a field gate. Through this gate our route turns right, up the ridge to a field gate on the right that is just past where the row of trees come up from the left. Our route goes through this gate and turns immediately left to continue up to a field gate, at 3, that leads on to open moorland.

3.(882348) Through this gate our route goes on up the moor (SSW) and at the first fork continues on up the green track through the bracken (S), not on the smaller path to the right, and continues to the left, around The Punchbowl for over .5km to a fork at a scattering of small hawthorn trees at 4.

4.(881341) The left path goes ENE and our route takes the right fork (E) on a grass track through the bracken for about a further .5km to where it goes across another grass track and continues ESE, and downwards, to join a tarmac lane opposite a house called Folly at 5.

5.(889339) If the weather has become unpleasant or if it is required to shorten the route turn left on this lane which goes down into Winsford. Our route turns right on the lane but keeps fairly close to the hedge bank on the left as it moves away from the lane, to the first field gate on the left. Through this gate our route goes on to open moorland and continues ESE, upwards, on a grass track across open moorland on a bridleway that is occasionally marked with paint on the top of isolated posts and which arrives at a small gate at 6.

6.(902332) Our route goes through this gate and across the lower side of the field, to a disused small quarry near the far side of which there is a field gate into the wood on the left. Through this gate our route forks to the left after a few metres to follow a bridleway down through the wood, frequently near the right bank of the brook, to just past a cottage that is on the opposite side of the brook at Yellowcombe. Here our route goes over the footbridge across the brook, over the stile and turns right to go through a field gate and continue on a track for about 1km to a lane in Winsford. Our route turns right on the lane back to the car park at 1.

Away from the village of Winsford this route goes through a valley of pastoral farmland and then climbs around the edge of The Punchbowl to go on to open moorland. The views from above The Punchbowl are very good and become more of a typical moorland scene after Folly. The return route to Winsford is then mainly through a wooded valley.

Tarr Steps, River Barle, Knaplock, Caratacus Stone and Varle Hill.

10km (6 miles).
The scenery is very good. The route includes some rolling farm land, a wooded river valley and moorland.
Can be muddy in winter.
Some modest slopes.
Overall from 210 metres up to 375 metres.
On certain days there is a bus to Tarr Steps.
Parking is possible at 1.
There is a tearoom at Tarr Steps and there is a pub at Withypool.

From Dulverton on the B3223 towards Exford turn left about 5km (3 miles) from Dulverton on to the lane to Tarr Steps that is immediately after a cattle grid. There is an Exmoor National Park car park on the left at 1, about 2km from this junction and just before Tarr Steps.

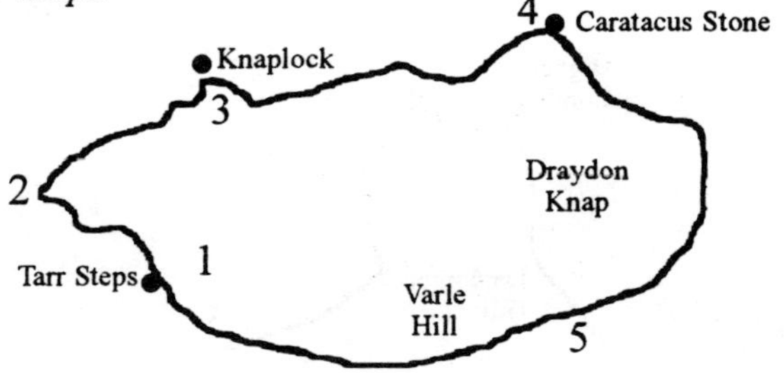

1.(872323) Our route goes down the lane, or down the footpath just to the right, to Tarr Steps where it turns right to continue up the right river bank, on a footpath or a bridleway, for about 1km to go through a field gate immediately following a footbridge over a stream that flows into the River Barle at 2.

2.(862326) Through the field gate our route turns right to go up a track for about 1km to the farm at Knaplock. Passing through Knaplock our route follows the track around to the right and about 100m from the right bend our route turns up to the left from Higher Knaplock at 3.

3.(870331) Our route follows the most obvious track up and away from Higher Knaplock. The track curves to the right and continues for just over 1km to a lane. Here our route turns left and is on the moorland on the right side of the lane for just under 500m to a crossroads at 4.

4.(888335) At the crossroads our route goes over the road and continues diagonally to the right to the small stone building that houses the Caratacus Stone and then bears right to continue on the track around the edge of the moorland. Our route follows the track near the left side of the moorland to a road at 5.

5.(892321) Here our route goes directly across the road on to an unfenced lane and continues along the lane to just past the first cattle grid. Here our route leaves the lane and goes through the first field gate and on to a track that soon forks. Our route takes the right fork for about 2km towards Tarr Steps, going through a field gate on the way. When the track drops down off the moor there are a few lesser tracks and paths crossing our route which comes to a field bank where, a few metres to the right, there is a small gate. Our route goes through this and down to Tarr Steps to follow the signed path or the lane back to the car park.

Winsford, Kemps, Higher Combe, River Exe and Bye Hill.

13km (8 miles) or 9km (6 miles).
The scenery is very good. A walk over rolling farmland and through the moorland valley of the Exe.
Usually good walking all year round.
Overall from 200 metres up to 375 metres.
Some modest slopes.
Winsford is on a regular summer bus route and an occasional all year bus route.
There is a car park at 1.
There is a tearoom and a pub at Winsford.

On the A396 between Dunster and Bridgetown turn right about 1km before Bridgetown on to a minor road signed to Winsford. There is a car park in Winsford, at 1, between the tearooms and the garage.

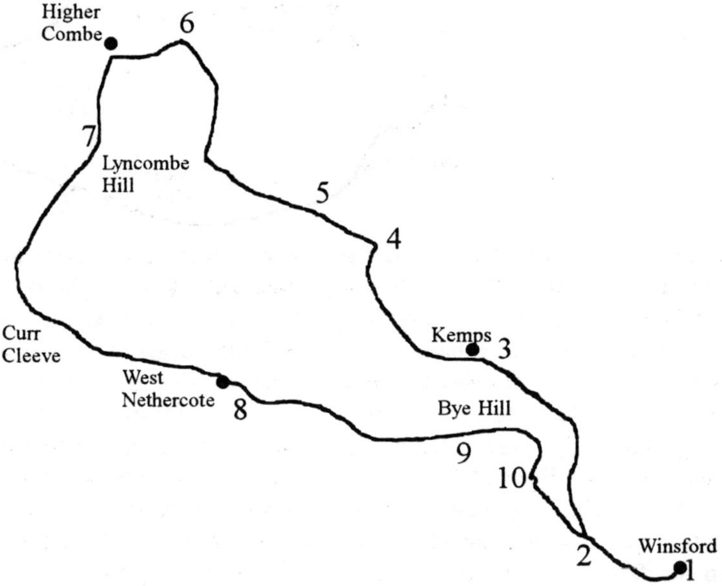

1.(906350) From the car park our route goes around the front of the tearooms, over the stone bridge next to the ford by the studio and continues up the lane for about 500m to go past the church which is on the right. About 500 metres up the lane from the ford the first signed footpath on the right goes through a field gate at 2.

2.(901351) Through the gate our route follows this path, keeping to the right when it forks at about 100m from the gate, and remains near the river for over a kilometre to arrive at a field gate. Through this gate our route turns right on the track to go over the bridge and on to the lane at 3.

3.(895363) Here our route turns left to go

over the bridge and up the track past Kemps Farm and continues on up the track for about 1.5km, through a few gates, to a T-junction at 4.

4.(886370) Here our route turns left to a field gate. Through this gate our route continues directly across the left side of the field to another field gate and on to a lane at 5.

5.(882372) Our route goes directly on to this lane and continues on it for just over 1km as it goes around the field to a field gate and then down between two hedges to the first track on the left at 6.

6.(874382) Here our route turns left down the track and continues around the buildings on the left near Higher Combe, then through a field gate and down the right side of a field to another field gate. Through this gate our route continues down the track and goes between the farm buildings at Lyncombe at 7.

7.(868375) After Lyncombe our route follows the track to a field gate and from this gate continues across the field, going slightly uphill, to follow a track that can vaguely be seen to go across to the field gate in the opposite hedge. From this gate our route goes directly on across the field, with the River Exe down on the right, to another field gate and from here continues on the same track for about 2km to go through the next farm, which is West Nethercote, and continues to go over the bridge across the River Exe. Our route remains on the track for about another 50 metres to the first track off to the right at 8.

8.(877361) Our route goes up this track and at the first field gate, about 50m up from the river, keeps to the left of the hedge bank to continue up to, and through, another field gate and then on up, near the hedge bank, to the next field gate on the right. Through this gate our route follows a marked bridleway directly away from the gate and near the fence for about 1km to arrive at a field gate across the bridleway at 9.

9.(889358) Through this gate our route continues along the track until it begins to move away from the wall on the right. Here our route leaves the track and continues on the path close to the wall to go through a small gate. Our route is close to the wall for about 750m to where there is a small wood ahead and a small gate on the right at 10.

10.(897357) Our route goes through the small gate, turns left to go through the next small gate, continues along the top of the wood and then turns left down the far side to the small gate on the right. Through this gate our route follows the path for about 500m to return to the lane and then turns left back to Winsford.

Short Route.

Where the field side path joins the lane at 5 our route turns left down the lane to go through Staddon Farm and continues down the marked bridleway to follow the track as it curves to the left near the bottom of the slope to go between East and West Nethercote and then on to the bridge over the river. About 50m after the bridge there is a track up to the right. This is at 8 and from here the notes can be followed as above.

Lucott Moor, Tarr Ball Hill and Chetsford Water.

Travelling towards Lynmouth, on the A39, from Porlock turn left about 3km (2 miles) from Porlock on to a minor road signed to Exford. About 5km (3 miles) along this minor road there is a small road bridge over a brook and the road bears left to go up the hill. Part of the way up the hill there are two small parking areas on the right in what are probably disused quarries, at 1.

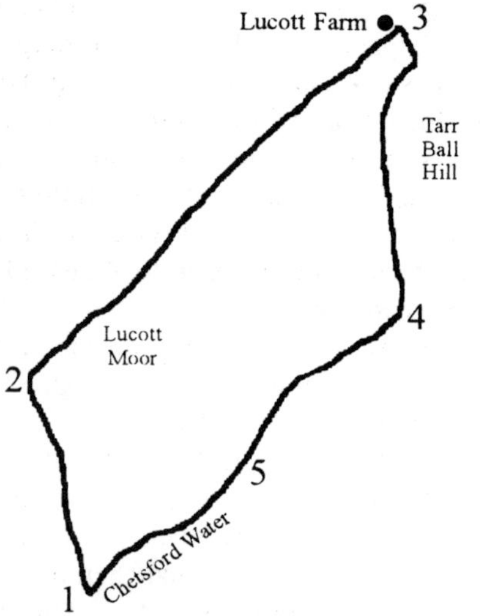

1.(848420) From the car park our route goes back down to the bridge and up the lane for just over 1km to a track opposite the first lane on the left, at 2.

2.(846432) Here our route turns right on to the track and across the moor for about .5km to go through a field gate and turn right, around the right side of the field, to the far right corner. Our route continues directly on through a field gate to follow a track across, and then between fields, for about 1.5km to Lucott Farm at 3.

3.(866450) Just where the farm buildings

8km (5 miles).
The scenery is very good. The walk is over some of the best viewpoints of Exmoor and offers some of the best views of Dunkery as well as the contrast of moorland and river valley.
Good walking all year round but after heavy winter rain some agility may be required to avoid wet feet.
Some modest slopes.
Overall from 247 metres up to 463 metres.
There is no public transport to this walk.
There are car parks at 1.
There are tearooms and pubs at Exford, Horner and Porlock.

end our route follows a track off to the right, down to the river, over the footbridge and then right on the first path that goes up past a cottage and then up a track to join another track that comes up from the valley. Our route continues up the track to go through the field gate and out on to the moor. Immediately at the first left bend our route turns off the track on to a path on the right at 4.

4.(866440) This path approximately follows the contour for about half a kilometre and then comes to a narrow tarmac lane. Turning left on this for about 30m our route then turns right on to another track and continues for about 1km to go gradually down to a ford at 5.

5.(859427) Our route goes across the ford and then turns left to continue upstream near the right bank of Nutscale Water but if the water is too deep to ford it should be possible to continue up the left bank until a crossing point is found. From here on our route continues up the valley. Just over half a kilometre up from the ford another brook, Embercombe Water, comes in from the left. Our route continues up the same valley near to, and occasionally crossing, the brook that is now called Chetsford Water to reach the bridge just below the car park..

Exford, Room Hill, Lyncombe and The River Exe.

10km (6 miles)
The scenery is very good. There are some very good views over Exmoor which contrast with the river valley.
Overall from 230 metres up to 375 metres.
On certain days there is a bus service to Exford.
There is a car park at 1.
There are tearooms and pubs in Exford.

On the B3224 travelling from Simonsbath to Wheddon Cross there is a car park on the right in Exford, at 1, after the bridge, filling station and shop.

1.(854384) From the far end of the car park our route continues on the path along the right side of two fields to go through a small gate and to turn right on to a track that goes across the bridge over the river. Over the bridge our route continues on the track to turn left on a lane that runs near to the far side of an old farm building and then between the farmhouse on the left and a bungalow on the right. When the track turns abruptly right to go around the bungalow our route keeps straight on, through a field gate and along a track with a field hedge on the left. Our route goes around the left side of the field to go through a field gate and continues on the track between the fence and the hedge to arrive at a field gate in the corner at 2.

2.(855376) Through this gate our route turns left, down between the hedge and the fence, to go through a small gate and continue down the track, over the small brook and up the track as it goes along the left side of the rough area and then through a field gate. Through this gate our route goes across the field, through another field gate, and then turns right up through some bracken and near the right side of the field to go through a gap where a row of beech trees goes off to the left. Our route continues across the right side of the field to go through a field gate and

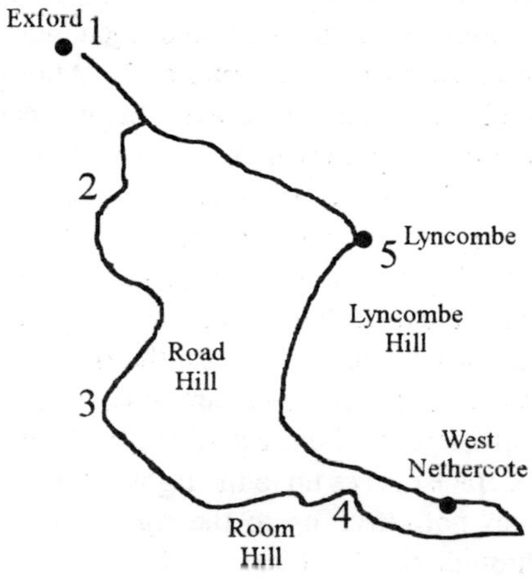

on, across the right side of a rough area on a track for about 200m to where the track forks at 3.

3.(856367) Our route follows the left fork for about 200m. Here, in theory an unmarked path turns off to the left to go across the gully and to continue approximately south east. The gully might be difficult for an inexperienced and less than agile walker to cross at any time of the year except in a dry summer. The most used route, which is not a public right of way, continues along the track, around the fenced area on the left, and then follows the line of the path over to the other side of the field to just before the hedge bank. Here our route turns left to follow a track that goes down through some small trees to the ford across the River Exe at 4.

4.(869363) If you prefer to cross the ford then on the other side our route follows the path up the side of the field to join another path. Here our route turns left and continues for about 1.5km as the path continues through the river valley, first through a rough area and then across some fields to Lyncombe at 5. Alternatively our route is down the riverside permissive path which continues through the field on the right side of the river, through a field gate and on to go through a small gate that leads on to a track. Here our route turns left on the track to go over the bridge and remains on the track as it curves to the left, goes through a farm and then there is a field gate directly ahead as the track curves up to the right. Our route does not curve up to the right but goes through the field gate and follows this track between the farm buildings at West Nethercote and on for about 2km to the next small farm which is Lyncombe, at 5.

5.(868375) Our route follows the track between the farm buildings to leave the yard by the field gate on the opposite side. Through this gate our route turns almost immediately left to go through another field gate and then across the field. There is a post marked path off to the right that avoids a lot of the mud and goes around to the left far side of the field where our route goes over a stile, over a small footbridge, and then over two more stiles. From here our route follows a path across some fields keeping just up from the river to go through a field gate and continue in the same direction, with a hedge bank now on the left, and then to follow the path as it curves up and to the right to the stile next to the field gate in the far right corner. Over the stile our route follows the track down the right side of the field to go through a small gate, across the track, through another small gate and then along the left side of the fields to return to the car park.

For all of the books published by The Moor, Dale and Mountain Press the policy is the same. First, a lot of time is spent walking the area and then, if, and only if, there are suitable paths and very good and contrasting rural scenery the walks are put into a book.

The aim is not to publish the maximum number of walks for any area. The aim is to publish the best.

Exford, Prescott and Prescott Down.

5km (3 miles).
The scenery is good. This walk is over rolling farmland and moorland with fairly extensive views.
Can be walked all year.
Overall from 260 metres up to 420 metres.
On certain days there is a bus service to Exford.
There is a car park at 1.
There are tearooms and pubs in Exford.

On the B3224 travelling from Simonsbath to Wheddon Cross there is a car park on the right in Exford, at 1, after the bridge, filling station and shop.

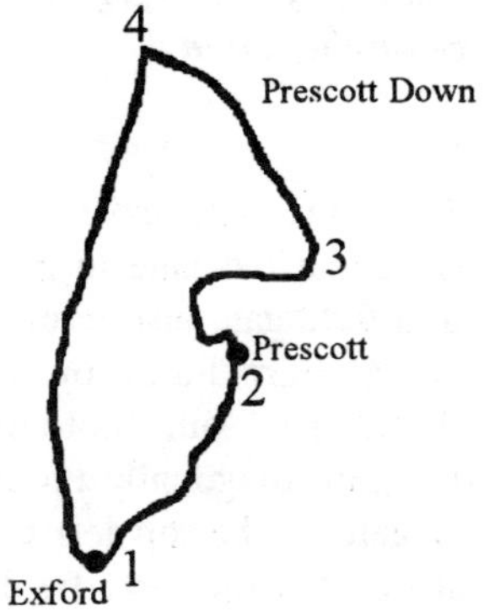

1.(854384) From the car park our route goes back on to the road and turns right for about 30m to follow the footpath on the left that goes up to the left of the houses and through a small gate and then almost directly across the field to a stile. Over the stile our route goes across the field and down to the far left corner, through a small gate and then turns left over the brook and through a field gate. Through the field gate our route turns right to go around the right side of the field, through a field gate in the corner and along a track to where the gardens on the right end. Here our route goes over the brook, over the stile and up the left side of the field to go over another stile and to continue up a field keeping slightly to the left of the ridge to arrive at a stile a few metres to the right of a field gate at 2.

2.(860391) Over the stile our route continues up the left side of the field and keeps to the left to go down a track and then continues between the ruined buildings at Prescott to bear left over the bridge. Past the bridge our route follows the track between the wood and the gorse and, when the gorse on the right ends, continues up the slope, keeping slightly to the right, to a field gate in the opposite hedge. Through the gate our route turns right for about 100m to follow a path signed to Prescott Down around the right side of the field as far as some steps over the bank. Our route goes over the steps into a field and continues up the right side of the field to the top right corner where there are two gateways. Our route goes through the left field gate and out on to the moor and continues directly up to a track on which it turns left at 3.

3.(863395) Our route follows the track for just over 1km to go across the moor, through a field gate, between two hedges and on to a field gate on the left that has a fingerpost pointing through it at 4.

4.(857404) Through the gate our route follows the track down to the field gate in the bottom right corner and through this continues on the track down the left side of the field. The track goes through two field gates and, near Exford, becomes a tarmac lane. When this lane joins a road at a T-junction our route turns left to go back through Exford to the car park.

Tarr Farm, Knaplock, River Barle and Tarr Steps.

From Dulverton on the B3223 towards Exford turn left about 6km (4 miles) from Dulverton, just after a cattle grid, on to a lane signed to Tarr Steps. About 2km down this lane there is an Exmoor Park car park on the left at 1.

8km (5 miles).
The scenery is very good. A walk over rolling farmland, over moorland and through the wooded valley of the River Barle.
Usually good walking all year round but can be slightly muddy in winter over two short sections. The riverside path can be difficult after heavy prolonged rains in winter and could be dangerous at one point following prolonged storms in winter.
Overall from 210 metres up to 360 metres.
Some modest slopes.
On certain days there is a bus to Tarr Steps.
There is a car park at 1.
There is a tearoom at Tarr Farm and there is a pub at Withypool.

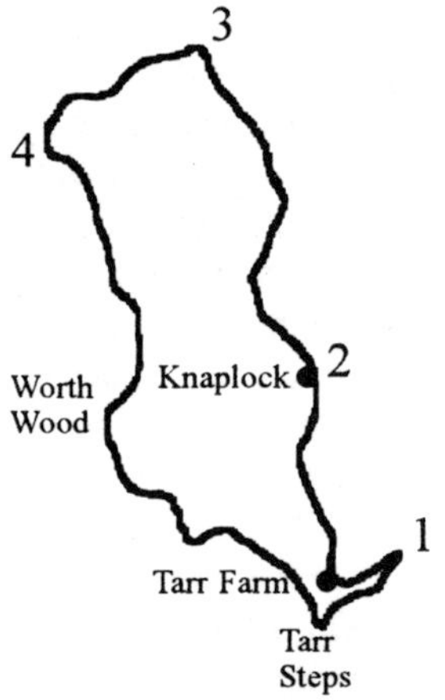

1.(872324) Our route leaves the car park and goes down the lane to a track that goes up to field gate just before the farm buildings at Tarr Farm on the right. Through the gate our route follows a track that goes diagonally up and to the left to a gate in the top left corner and continues across the next field keeping on up and slightly to the left to a field gate about half way along the hedge bank at the top of the field. Through this gate our route goes across a narrow field keeping slightly to the right, not to the gate that can be seen in the far right corner but the field gate hidden under a tree trunk about 75m to the left of it. Through this gate our route continues across the right side of the field to go through the first field gate on the right and then goes immediately through the field gate on the left into the corner of a field. From here our route goes diagonally down the field to go through the gate in the bottom corner and continues along the bottom of the next field for about 25m to the first field gate on the left. Through this gate our route goes down and across the field towards the right hand side of the stone buildings to go through a field gate, over a small bridge across the brook and across a track to continue up a track that runs between the old stone buildings of Knaplock on the left and the steel barn on the right, to a field gate at 2.

2.(868331) Through this field gate our route keeps to the left on an old track until the track comes down to a field gate through which our route comes to a narrow stretch of moorland through which a brook flows. Our route turns right, up the left side of the moorland on a track that bends around to the left. Soon after this left bend it is very easy to go the wrong way and follow the track around to the right but our route stays near to the hedge bank on the left to open moorland. Our route then continues along the edge of the moorland, with a field bank on the left, for about 1km to some farm buildings on the left at 3.

3.(861344) Our route turns left through a field gate by the side of a cattle grid and goes down the lane for about 250m to a small gate on the right just before the lane bends to the right. Our route goes through the small gate, across the field with a relic of a field bank on the left, through another small gate and into a wood. Our route follows the path down through the wood and over a brook from where our route continues on a track that continues down and above, the right bank of the brook to the River Barle at 4.

4.(857339) Here our route turns left to continue on a path that is near the left bank of the River Barle to Tarr Steps. At Tarr Steps our route continues across the lane to go over the first stile on the left which is about 20m before a field gate. Over the stile our route follows the footpath up the valley and above the right side of the brook to go over a footbridge and back to the car park at 1.

Every walk in every book or booklet published by The Moor, Dale and Mountain Press is selected on the quality and extent of the natural scenery.

Although every walker's opinion of local scenery may vary there would probably not be a lot of different opinions when comments are requested on the scenery in terms of "pleasant, good or the very best." Included in this booklet are comments on the natural scenery and they range from pleasant to the very best in the order of pleasant, good, very good, outstanding or the very best.

A walk that simply went across rural farmland, however varied, and through a small wood would not be good enough to be included. A walk that offered more than this could be included and described as pleasant.

Hawkridge, Venford Moor, Dane's Brook and Hawkridge Ridge.

On the B3223, Dulverton to Exford, turn left on to the first minor road and over a bridge about 1km from Dulverton. About 3km (2 miles) along this minor road turn right on to a lane signed to Hawkridge. Parking is possible on the right just before the telephone kiosk at 1.

9km (6 miles).
The scenery is very good. This is a walk over moorland, through riverside woodland and over some farmland.
Can be muddy in winter.
Overall from 175 metres up to 350 metres.
Some modest slopes.
There is no public transport to this walk.
Parking is possible in Hawkridge at 1.
There are no pubs or tearooms on this walk.
There is a tearoom at Tarr Steps and there is a pub at Withypool.

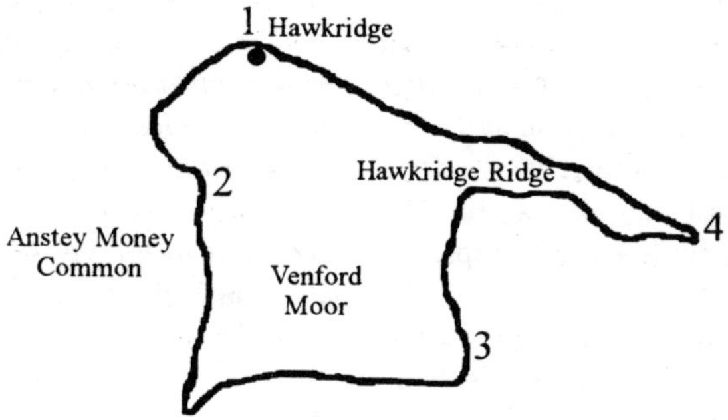

1.(861306) From the parking area our route follows the lane away from the church and the telephone kiosk as it curves down and to the left to where the lane bends sharp right. A few metres past this bend a bridleway goes through the field gate on the left and this is also signed as the route of the long distance path, the Two Moors Way, with the M over the W. Our route follows the Two Moors Way across the field to go just to the right of the tree stump and then curves slightly to the right to go through a field gate and on to a lane where our route turns left on the lane, down across the bridge and up the other side of the valley for about 100m to 2 where the Two Moors Way is waymarked to go off to the right opposite a field gate from which a track leads down to a conifer plantation.
2.(859301) Our route follows the Two Moors Way as it curves up and to the left across the moor. When it is crossed by another track our route keeps on going up to join and turn right on a track on the moorland side of a field bank. When this

track comes to a minor road our route leaves the Two Moors Way and turns left, past the first field gate and then goes through the small gate on the left. Through this gate our route continues around the left side of the area of shrubs and gorse on the right to where a well used track goes off to the right with a large patch of gorse on the left of it. Our route goes over this track and to the left of the patch of gorse until less than 100m from a field bank where our route turns right to follow a path that is almost parallel with the field bank to a small gate at the far side of the field. Through this field gate our route continues in approximately the same direction for about 500m to go through a field gate on the left and then directly across a lane. Across the lane our route goes through the field gate and keeps slightly to the right to follow the path and to go through a small gate at 3.

3.(871291) Through this small gate one path continues almost directly on along the top of the field and another goes slightly to the left. Our route follows the one that goes down and slightly to the left to continue through a gap in a row of trees and down the right side of the valley to a footbridge. Over the footbridge our route goes slightly uphill and then curves down and to the right on a path that goes down the left bank of Dane's Brook to near a stone bridge at 4.

4.(884296) Here our route turns left on a track that doubles back on, and above, the route to the bridge. Our route continues up the ridge to a field gate through which our route then continues near the ridge and across some fields. When the fields end our route follows the track through a field gate and between two hedges into Hawkridge.

This is a walk of much contrast within quite a small area of Exmoor. Hawkridge is a quiet Exmoor hamlet that is away from the main roads and after leaving Hawkridge our path goes across the valley of Dane's Brook and is soon on open moorland with good local scenery across, and along, the valley.

Across an area of Access Land, which is more scrub than moorland, our path then enters the old deciduous woods that fill the valley through which Dane's Brook flows to join the River Barle.

Some people find the path that goes up the ridge and through the wood to be the best part of the walk with the rock outcrops, the two rivers, the views over and through the trees but throughout the few square kilometers of the entire walk the extent of the contrast is typical of that which can be found on Exmoor.

Molland, Gourt Mires and Smallacombe.

On the A361, South Molton to Bampton, turn left about 9km (5 miles) from S. Molton on to a minor road signed to Molland. Continue past Molland Church for about 250m to where the road bends left. Turn off here to continue directly on for about 400m and then turn left on to the no through lane for about 750m to just before where the tarmac lane bends sharp right. It should be possible to park off the road here, on the left.

6km (4 miles).
The scenery is very good. The route includes rolling farmland, a river valley and moorland.
Can be muddy in winter.
Some modest slopes.
Overall from 190 metres up to 330 metres.
There is no public transport to this walk.
Parking is possible at 1.
There is a pub at Molland and tearooms at Exford and South Molton.

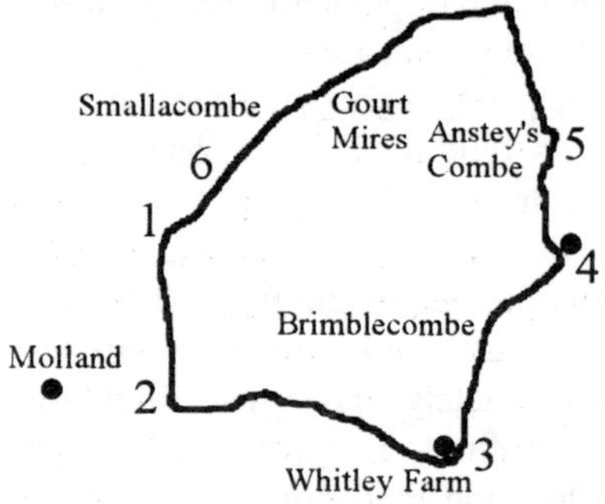

1.(814290) Our route goes back to the junction, turns left over a stile to go across the top of three fields with a bank on the left and then continues down across the next field to a stile on to a lane. On the lane our route turns left for about 250m to the first sharp right bend at 2.
2.(819282) Here our route leaves the lane to continue directly on along a track to Whitley Farm where our route follows the track through a field gate, past the house on the left and to another field gate at 3.
3.(827281) Through this field gate our route turns left on the track down into the valley and continues near the left bank of the stream to a field gate where there is a small ford on the right. Our route goes over the ford and through a field gate to continue between the wood and the stream for about 200m to join another path. Here our route continues slightly to the left and gradually climbs out of the valley on a path between two banks to Brimblecombe at 4.
4.(831288) At Brimblecombe our route joins a track and keeps to the left of the buildings to go through a field gate and continue up a track which bears left after about 200m to go across the fields and on to the moorland at 5.
5.(830293) *If the visibility is poor it may be preferable to turn left on to the bridleway that runs along the edge of the moorland for about 1.5km to 6.* Our route continues up and slightly to the right, on to the moor and as far as where the first broad bridleway bears off to the left. Here our route bears off to the left to continue slightly uphill along the right hand side of a combe and then bears left across the top of the combe. Then our route continues across the top of a smaller combe to join another track on which our route turns left. Our route follows this track above a combe that progressively deepens on the right to near the edge of the moor where the track goes down into the combe to cross a shallow ford, to go over a small bridge and to reach a field gate at the edge of the moor at 6.
6.(816291) Here our route goes through the field gate and on to a lane back to 1.

Larkbarrow, Long Combe, Trout Hill, River Exe and Elsworthy.

Travelling towards Lynmouth on the A39 from Porlock turn left about 3km (2 miles) from Porlock on to a minor road signed to Exford. About 4km (3 miles) along this minor road turn right on to another minor road at Lucott Cross. Just over 2km along this minor road the hedge on the right ends, there is a field gate and a small gate and there are parking spaces along the road next to the fenced bank at 1.

13km (8 miles)
The scenery is very good. The walk is through moorland scenery throughout and is probably about as far from crowds and into Exmoor as it is possible to get. For a large part of the walk there are no paths but it would be extremely difficult to get lost.
Part of this walk is extremely wet and muddy over the top of the moorland except at the drier times of the year.
Some modest slopes.
Overall from 330 metres up to 435 metres.
There is no public transport to this walk.
There is a car park at 1.
There are tearooms and pubs at Exford and Porlock.

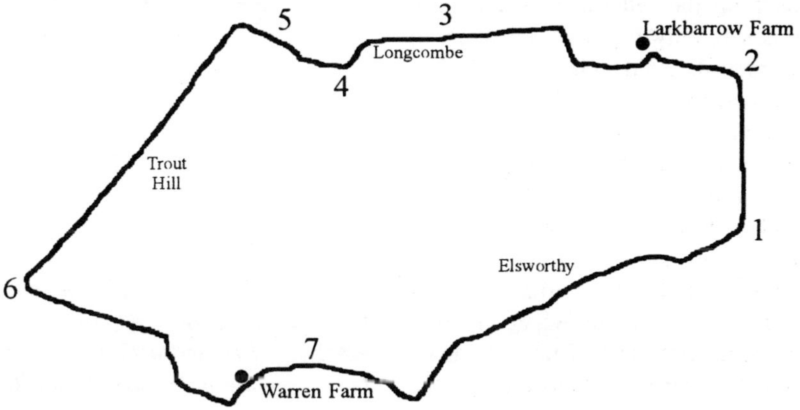

1.(827418) From the end of the parking space our route goes through the small gate on to the Access Land that is owned by Exmoor National Park. There is a display board that indicates that walkers have freedom to roam within the boundary. Our route continues directly along the track for about 1km to go through a field gate at 2.

2.(827428) Our route then follows the track around to the left and on through gates, and past ruins on the right, to come to a field gate where the track leaves the fields and goes on to open moorland at 3.

3.(808430) There is a fingerpost that points directly on from the gate and along the track but our route bears left on an unsigned path that curves gently down towards the stream for about 500m to cross a footbridge just past where two

streams join at 4.
4.(803428) Over the footbridge our route follows the path that can be seen to go up and to the right but this path soon fades as our route continues across the rough grass between the ridge on the left, and the stream, for about 600m to then go down towards the stream to where another stream comes in from the left to join the main stream at 5.
5.(797430) Here our route goes over the smaller stream that comes in from the left and then our route goes directly up the hill and bears slightly to the left to continue over the brow to a fence that runs approximately up the ridge of Trout Hill. Our route turns left at the fence and continues up the hill for almost 2.5km. The fence is only a guide. There is an animal track alongside it but all of the hill is open to walkers. Near the top of the hill the fence joins another fence on what was once a stone bank and here our route turns left at 6.
6.(780415) In winter the drier parts are probably either about 10m out from the fence or on top of the remains of the old wall for about .5km to where another bank goes off to the left. This area can be very muddy. Our route goes through the field gate on the right and for some of the best views along the valley of the River Exe our route goes diagonally on and down to the right, avoiding the wetter parts. There is a stile where a fence comes down to the river and there is a field gate about 50m above the stile. Through this gate and down a few metres there is a path that continues across the slope, above the river, to arrive at a field gate on to a lane. Our route turns left on the lane and when the lane turns abruptly left in to Warren Farm continues on through the small gate on to a track. Our route follows the track up and then right, across the top of two fields to go through a field gate and on to the moor at 7.
7.(799409) Here our route continues directly on a track, across moorland fields or open moorland, near to a field bank on the right, to a field gate where the field bank on the right bears sharply away to the right. Our route follows the track through the gate and over the open moorland for about a further 1.5km to where the track meets a bank and turns sharp right down to a gate and then on down to the lane where our route turns left, back to 1.

For the Exmoor book the amount of tarmac that has been included is extremely low and with most of the walks there is none apart from, usually, just a small amount to or from the car park at the starting point. There seemed to be little point in producing a book of walks for places where it is possible to drive.

Scenic contrast is very high on the list of priorities when walks are being selected for publication and there are probably very few areas of the U.K. that can offer such contrast over comparatively small areas as does Exmoor.

Simonsbath, River Barle, Cow Castle, Picked Stones and Winstitchen.

Travelling towards Dulverton from Lynmouth on the B3223 there is an Exmoor National Park car park at Ashcombe, at 1, in Simonsbath just past the Exmoor Forest Hotel on the left.

12km (8 miles) or 9km (6 miles).
The scenery is very good. This walk includes the valley of the River Barle, some moorland and returns on some high ground overlooking the valley.
Can be walked all year round.
Some modest slopes and a steep one on the short route.
Overall from 275m up to 397m.
On certain days of the week there is a bus service to Simonsbath.
There is a car park at 1.
There are tearooms and a pub in Simonsbath.

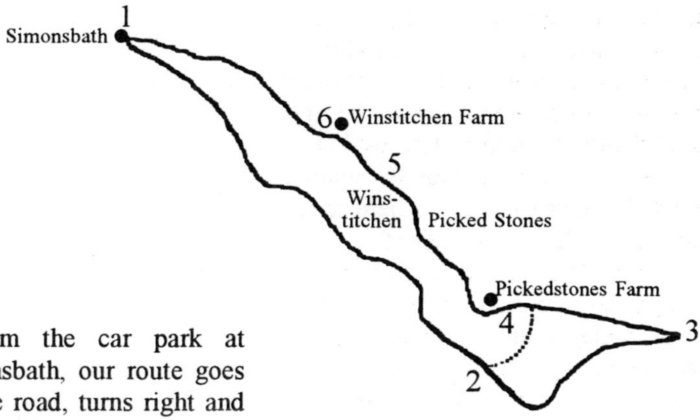

1.(774394) From the car park at Ashcombe, Simonsbath, our route goes back out on to the road, turns right and goes past the hotel and then the pottery shop to turn left across the road and on to the footpath which is signed through the small gate and into the wood. This path remains in the river valley and is usually quite close to the left side of the river for about 4km, where it leaves a conifer wood at 2. On the way down the river curves off to the right, twice, to go around two small hills and although a small path does follow the riverbank our route keeps to the left of both hills to subsequently rejoin the riverbank.

2.(803367) Through the gate at the end of the conifer wood our route continues on a track across a rough slope and then through a field gate where the track continues up and slightly to the left to cross the heath. About 1.5km from the gate the track curves slightly left between some gorse bushes and then goes through a gap in a low ancient field bank. Directly ahead is an area of heather and the track curves right. Our route turns left on to another track here, at 3.

3.(819370) To begin with the track remains near the right side of the ancient field bank and is then very obvious as it continues in virtually the same direction for just over 1km to leave the heath through a field gate. Through the gate our route continues across the field to go through another field gate and out on to a track on which our route turns left at 4.

4.(803372) Our route follows this track

around the left side of Pickedstones Farm and then bears right, around a field, and on for about 1km on the track that is occasionally paint waymarked to the bridge at Picked Stones. Across the bridge our route follows the waymarks and the track around the disused quarry and up the left side of the field to where the track turns left into the adjacent field at 5.

5.(794381) Our route continues along the left side of the small conifer plantation and around the right side of this field, and the next two fields, to arrive at a field gate. Through this gate our route turns right to go down the right side of the field and turns left just before the field gate on to the lane to continue around the right side of the field to the small gate in the next corner at 6.

6.(783389) Our route goes through this small gate and continues across the right side of some fields to a field gate that leads into the left side of a field. Across the left side of the field our route then goes through a field gate and directly on for about 30m to go through another field gate and down the right side of the field to another field gate. Through this gate our route goes down and to the left to go through the wood, which is Access Land, and on through a small gate opposite the hotel. Across the road our route turns right back to the car park.

Short route. Follow the notes through to 2(803367) and just through the field gate across the track turn left to go up the steep slope. The path here is rather vague because it has been little used. There is a small gate into the field above and it is to the left of the gap between the gorse and the rock outcrop. Our route goes through this small gate and continues on for a few metres and then turns right to be near the right side of the hedge bank. Again the route of the footpath is a little vague but just before the far left corner there is a field gate on the left and through this gate and almost directly up the field our route goes through a field gate and continues on for about 30 metres to be level with a field gate on the right. Here our route turns left to continue almost directly across the field to go through a field gate and to turn left on a track at 4.

Each of the walks in this series from The Moor, Dale and Mountain Press is a circular walk that can be started at a number of places with the minimum need to walk the same paths twice.

The Doone Valley, Badgworthy Water, Brendon Common and Malmsmead Hill.

10km (6 miles).
The scenery is outstanding. The walk is through the heart of "Doone Country" with the contrast of a river valley with some moorland and heath from which there are very good views over much of Exmoor.
Good walking all year round but there are some small fords and one, at 4, that might be difficult to cross if there has been continuous rain over the preceeding forty eight hours.
Some modest slopes.
Overall from 240 metres up to 399 metres.
There is no public transport to this walk.
Car parking is possible near 1.
There are tearooms at Malmsmead and Brendon and pubs at Rockford and Brendon.

Travelling towards Minehead on the A39 from Lynmouth turn right about 4km from Lynmouth on to a minor road signed to Brendon. In Brendon follow the road round to the right and across the bridge over the river to the crossroads. Continue over the crossroads on the minor road signed to Tippacott for just over 1km to turn left at a T-junction on the moor. About 1km down this lane a track that is a bridleway comes on to the road from the moor on the right at 1 and continues through a field gate on the left.

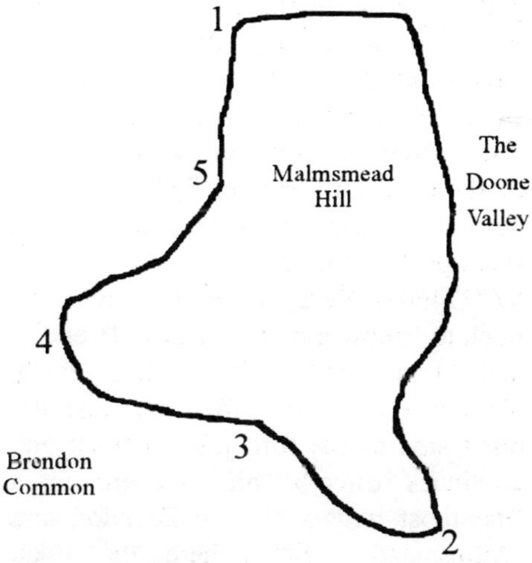

1.(782473) Our route continues down the lane for about 1km to where the lane bends left and a track goes off to the right, through a field gate and there is a path signed to the Doone Valley. Our route follows this track for about 3km to the second footbridge. There are some minor fords on the way and after about 2km a track bears off to the right through some trees but our route follows the track near the river bank to just before a footbridge that is the other side of a field gate in an old stone bank at 2.

2.(793444) Here our route does not cross the footbridge but bears right before the field gate and continues on a track that runs almost parallel with the stream on the left for about 100m and then continues, curving slightly to the right, on to open moorland where it is close to a redundant bank on the left for about 150m. Then our route follows the track as it curves to the right and then to the left for a total distance of just over 1.5km from 2 to reach a field gate at 3.

3.(781452) At virtually all times of the

year this section is quite straight forward as our route continues almost directly on in the same direction along what is not really definable as a track because it is slightly wet for much of the year and horse riders who use the area tend to spread out their route to avoid making it muddier. But if the clouds descend it can be difficult to see where the track is meant to be for the next 700m or so. From 3 the track heads approximately 300 degrees west to stay between the ridge on the left and the steep slope down to the brook on the right. After about 700m from 3 the track is very obvious and curves down to the right to cross a ford at 4.

4.(771456) This is Lankcombe Ford and on the other side of it there are numerous paths leading up the slope. Our route follows the most worn path that goes very slightly to the right (NNE) and up the slope for about 200m to join a broad track. Here our route turns right (ENE) on the track for just over 500m to where the track bears right and there is a fingerpost on the left at 5.

5.(777460) Here our route leaves the track to follow a path signed to Brendon and Malmsmead. The path is fairly obvious (NNE) to a ford and just the other side of the ford joins a track and continues directly on. There is a fingerpost with a sign to Brendon and Malmsmead. From here the track continues northward for about 750m, back to 1.

As with most hill areas in England the scenery on Exmoor changes from heath to moorland so that above 350 metres the scene from most of the hills is across the wild grasses, over heath and then to whatever is beyond.

This walk begins on the edge of pastoral farmland and goes down to the valley of Badgworthy Water. Part of Badgworthy Water has open aspects and then the river valley is wooded, with many old deciduous trees.

As our route follows the river above the wood the scene is very typically the Exmoor scene that is frequently portrayed by artists. Rounded hills of moorland colours, gentle valleys with a brook and with a few small trees. This is the heart of Doone Country: the merging of the gentler landscape with what can at times be the bleak wilderness of the exposed moor.

Our route goes past the deserted medieval settlement to rise above the derelict banks of what once were the small enclosed fields and progressively the scene becomes more rugged. Lost from view are the old trees of Badgworthy Water and now there is the exposed, windswept heath and moorland.

Brendon Two Gates, Lanacombe and Hoccombe Water.

5km (3 miles).
The scenery is very good with extensive views over unspoiled moorland.
For most of this walk there are no paths or tracks, other than animal tracks, and most of it is over rough moorland grassland.
After heavy winter rain this area can be very boggy but can be walked all year round.
Some modest slopes.
Overall from 380 metres up to 445 metres.
On certain days of the week there is a bus to Brendon Two Gates.
Car parking is possible near 1.
There is a tearoom and a pub at Simonsbath.

From Simonsbath follow the B3223 towards Lynmouth for just over 4km (3 miles) to Brendon Two Gates at the Somerset and Devon Border. Just before the cattle grid at the boundary there are parking spaces on the left at 1.

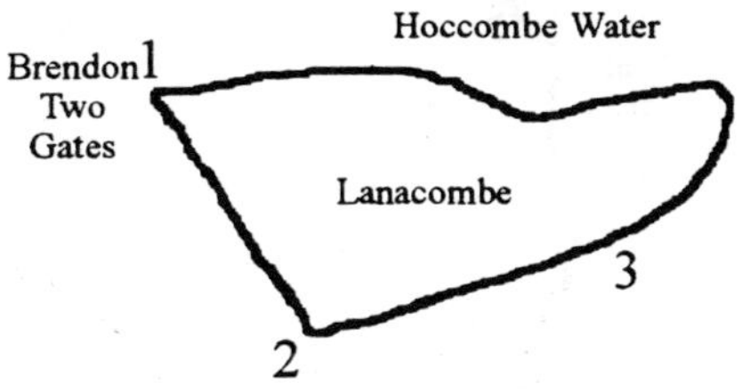

1.(765432) Over on the right, just before the cattle grid, there is a field gate and through this gate our route goes across the moorland towards 150 degrees and continues over the ridge until about 1km from 1 where our route joins a little used grass track at 2. (Without a compass it is possible to go through the gate, turn right and walk towards the ridge in a line just left of parallel with the road at this point and continue in the same direction when the road bears away to the right.)

2.(771424) Our route turns left on the track and after about 1km passes above an old disused enclosure with some beech trees growing near each corner at 3.

3.(782426) Our route continues towards 40 degrees and soon the track becomes even less distinct as our route follows approximately the same contour. In less than 1km our route bears left around the spur and remains on about the same contour to continue due west with the brook called Hoccombe Water down on the right. There are some animal tracks between the top of the steeper slope that comes up from the brook and the ridge and these can make for easier walking. Our route continues on about the same contour, and on the same side of Hoccombe Water. About 1.5km from the spur there is a gully that at times can be sufficiently wet to cause a slight detour but usually it is possible to cross it and then our route continues for about .5km back to 1.

Simonsbath, Prayway Head, Dure Down, Cornham and Burcombe.

Travelling towards Dulverton from Lynmouth on the B3223 there is an Exmoor National Park car park at Ashcombe, at 1, in Simonsbath just past the Exmoor Forest Hotel on the left.

11km (7 miles).
The scenery is outstanding. This walk includes some of the most contrasting and some of the most unspoiled areas of Exmoor.
Parts of this walk are over rough moorland grassland over which there are no paths at all.
In winter there are many very wet and muddy places but it can be walked all year round.
Some modest slopes.
Overall from 308 metres up to 480 metres.
On certain days of the week there is a bus service to Simonsbath.
There is a car park at 1 and another at 3.
There are tearooms and a pub in Simonsbath.

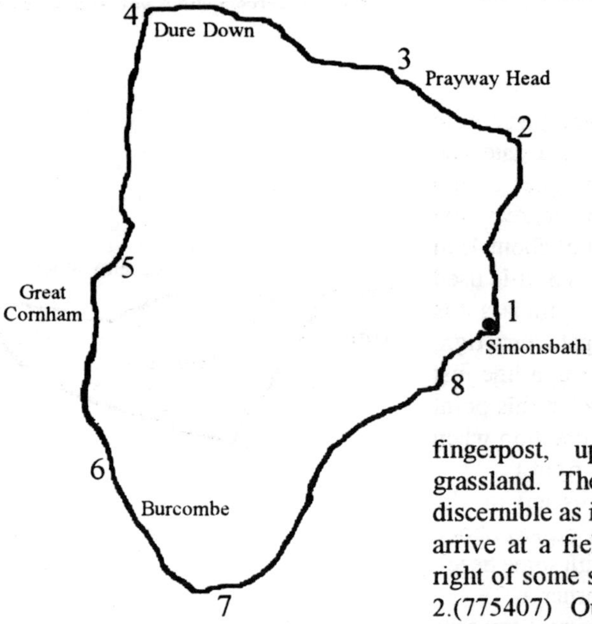

1.(774394) From the upper car park at Ashcombe our route follows a permissive footpath, signed to Prayway Head, up through the wood. At the end of the wood our route follows the footpath down to the left, across the brook, up through the fir trees and through a gate on the right into a field and then follows the marked footpath across the field to go through a small gate on to some rough ground. Our route goes around the rough ground keeping to the left of an old bank and then turns right, where there is a fingerpost, up through some rough grassland. The path can be vague but is discernible as it goes up and to the left to arrive at a field gate about 20m to the right of some sheep pens at 2.

2.(775407) Our route goes through this field gate and turns left on to an area of access land and continues for about 500m to a small gate on the left that is just past a field gate. Our route goes through the small gate and then turns right on the road verge for about 300m to a parking area on the left at 3.

3.(767411) There is a small gate off the parking area and our route goes through this gate and immediately turns right to go through another small gate near the corner. Through this small gate our route turns left on another area of Access Land

and continues on the right of the field bank to arrive at, and go directly through, a field gate. Through the gate our route bears to the right to go to the brow of Dure Down. From the brow our route continues approximately westwards to reach a field gate at an apex of the fences and where a track goes through the field gate at 4.

4.(750414) Through the gate our route turns immediately left to follow a permissive path down the left side of the field to go through a small gate and to continue on down the left side of the next field but keeping near the top of the combe. There are intermittent yellow topped posts that mark the path that goes down to and over a stile in the lower bank. Over the stile our route continues down the left side of the field, again the path does have intermittent yellow marker posts. At about the lowest point in the field there is a field gate on the left but our route follows the footpath past this gate and up and a little to the right to join a track that goes through a field gate where there is a fingerpost, at 5, signed to Cornham Farm.

5.(750399) Through this gate our route turns right. Up and to the left, about 500m away is Cornham Farm. Our route follows the footpath towards Cornham Farm to go through a field gate near the corner of the field. Through the field gate our route goes directly across the road and up the lane towards Cornham Farm where our route follows the track around the right side of the buildings to where it bends sharp left to go between the buildings. Here our route continues directly on, through a field gate, to follow a vague track across the field to another field gate. Through this gate our route follows a track down into the valley to go through another field gate and turn right to cross a very wet area to the footbridge at 6.

6.(749386) Over the footbridge our route continues directly on to join a track that continues up through the combe. The area on both sides of this track is Access Land. After about 1.25km the track arrives at a field gate on to a road. In summer it is probably preferable to turn left and go over the rough grassland to the first small gate on the right but this area is extremely wet in winter when it is probably preferable to go through the gate on to the road and turn left for about 200m to the field gate on the right that is just past the junction with a lane on the right and opposite the small gate at 7.

7.(758377) Our route goes through the field gate on the right and directly ahead there is an old ditch with banks that goes across the rough moorland and slightly to the left. All this area is Access Land. Our route follows these banks to some noticeable earthworks and then turns left (heading approx. 30 degrees) to follow some intermittent earthworks for about 750m to a fence. Here our route turns right, keeping about 75m above the fence to avoid the wetter areas, to the first field gate on the left. Our route goes through this gate and continues directly down the field to join a track on which our route turns right. Just before this track goes through the remains of a bank our route turns left for a few metres to go through the small gate on the right at 8.

8.(769389) Through this small gate our route goes diagonally down the slope to go around the far end of the wood and turn left on to a track which leads to a field gate on to a lane. Our route turns right on the lane and then right at the next junction to return to the car park at 1.

Chains Barrow, Wood Barrow and Moles Chamber.

On the B3358 heading towards Challacombe and about 5km (3 miles) from Simonsbath there is a car parking area along the right hand verge at 1.

1.(729401) From the small gate on the Simonsbath side of the car park our route follows a signed path up the right side of the field, through a field gate and directly on for about 250m to go through a field gate in the bank on the right and then continues generally northwards on a path marked with painted posts for just over 1km to a small gate in a field bank at 2.
2.(732418) (Chains Barrow is about 250m off our route. From the gate it is up the slope and to the right.) Through the gate our route turns left and with the field bank on the left goes past Pinkworthy Pond and up to a field gate. Through this gate our route goes up and to the right, towards Wood Barrow, at 3.
3.(716425) Just before Wood Barrow our route turns left to remain in the field and to follow a track that is near to the hedge bank on the right for just over 1.5km as it goes down, through a field gate on the way, to another field gate on to a road at 4.
4.(718409) Our route goes across the road, through a field gate and then follows the track until the hedge bank on the right turns abruptly right. Here our route leaves the track and turns left to continue in the same field and near the fence on the right. Our route goes through the next field gate and continues in about the same direction to go through another field gate at the end of the field, down across another field and through another field gate and then continues on a

9km (6 miles).
The scenery is good. Most of the walk is over moorland or marginal moorland farming.
This walk is in part over The Chains which is one of the few areas of Exmoor that is almost a wilderness. Can be walked all year but may be muddy in winter.
Overall from 364 metres up to 480 metres.
There are no bus services to this walk.
There is a car park at 1.
There are tearooms and pubs at Challacombe and Simonsbath.

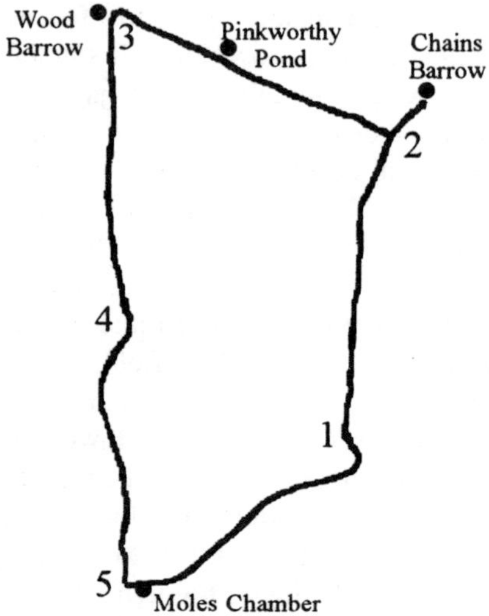

track for about 250m to where the fence on the left turns abruptly down towards the bottom of the valley. Here our route turns left to go through the field gate on the left in that fence, at 5.
5.(718394) Our route follows a vague track across the field as it gradually goes down to cross the brook in the far right corner and continues through a gate. From here on the path is on the right of the brook as it continues for about 200m to cross a narrow wet area and then continues on about the same contour to a field gate as the brook drops away to the left. Through this field gate our route continues in about the same direction on a track for about 500m to the road where our route turns left to the car park.

Shallowford, Furzehill Common, The Chains, Pinkworthy Pond and Saddle Gate.

About 7km (4 miles) from Lynmouth on the A39, heading towards Blackmoor Gate, there is a filling station on the left at Barbrook. Immediately past the filling station there is a small lane on the left. Follow this lane to the end where there is a small bridge just before Shallowford Farm. Before the tarmac ends it is usually possible to park off the lane at 1.

10km (7 miles).
The moorland scenery is very good. This is not a walk for an inexperienced walker. One of the few areas of Exmoor that is almost a wilderness.
Part of the walk is over an area of Access Land where there are no paths and which some people might find difficult. The Chains is one of the wettest areas on Exmoor and in winter is usually so waterlogged that this walk would not then be pleasant.
Some modest slopes.
Overall from 290 metres up to 460 metres.
There are no bus services to this walk.
Parking is usually possible at 1.
There are tearooms and pubs at Lynton and Lynmouth.

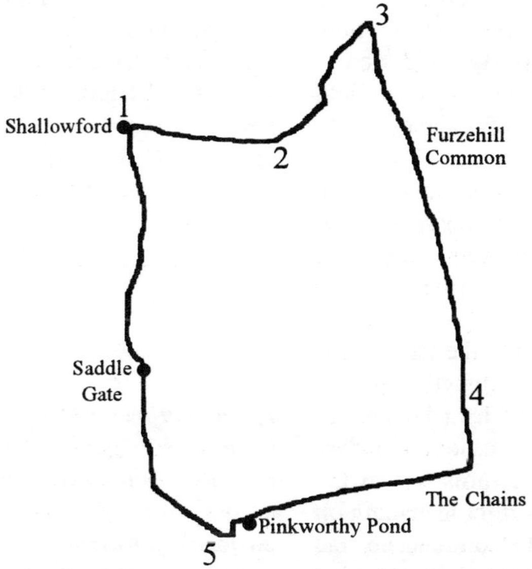

1.(714450) As the lane approaches Shallowford Farm the land immediately on the left is Access Land where walkers are free to roam. Just before the lane goes over the brook our route turns off across this Access Land and continues near the left bank of the brook for about 200m from where it heads due east (the lane runs approx. north-south). The path is across heath and Access Land so there is no need to be concerned with a distinct path. The point where our route leaves the heath is almost directly over the ridge and down the other side where a track goes through a field gate at Hill Cottage at 2.

2.(723449) Our route follows the track down and over a small brook and up past the farm and water wheel on the left to continue in almost the same direction on to a tarmac lane. About 200m along the lane, after going between the two houses, our route turns right through a field gate and up a track between two hedges. At the top of the track our route goes through the field gate and directly on to go through the small gate and up the left side of the field. Then our route goes through another field gate and across the left corner of the field to a field gate on the left at 3.

3.(729457) Our route does not go through this gate but turns right to follow the signed path across the field, across another field and across the next field keeping slightly to the left to go out on to the moor through a field gate. From this gate our route stays near to the hedge on the right until this hedge bears away to the right and here our route continues almost directly across the moor for about 400m to go through a field gate. Here the path is signed to go up to the left but our route continues almost directly on near the left side of the ditch and bank for about 750m to arrive at a field boundary bank. Here our route turns left to the corner and then bears right to remain on the open moor and to continue up and slightly to the left to the field gate that can be seen on the skyline at 4.

4.(740432) Through this gate our route continues almost directly on for a few metres to join a grass track that continues southwards, around the right side of the large gully on the left, to the top of the first hill. From here a large wet combe that goes down to the left can be seen. Here our route turns right across the rough grass and, avoiding the wet places, continues due west for about 1.5km to go around the top of the wet combe that goes down to the right and on to go past Pinkworthy Pond, which is down in the hollow on the left. Just before the field boundary our route turns left and continues down the moorland side of the field boundary to join a path and turn right to go through the field gate in the corner at 5.

5.(720423) Through this gate our route continues on the path across to another field gate in the far right corner and through this gate continues almost directly on a vague path approximately northwards. Progressively the path becomes more distinct and, keeping on the right of the combe that progressively forms on the left, goes through another field gate, which is Saddle Gate after about 1km. Through this field gate our route continues on the track back to 1.

From Shallowford the scene towards The Chains is a gentle heather slope that extends to the skyline. Our route goes across the heather, through some pastoral farmland to then follow a moorland path to the top of the hill. The view from the top of the hill is good over this part of The Chains, an area of moorland grasses that is as much a wilderness as England can offer. There is the occasional buzzard and there are many skylarks but usually most of the activity will be your own.

Minehead, North Hill, Bratton Ball and Burgundy Chapel.

From the A39 turn off into Minehead to the seafront and then north west along the seafront towards the old harbour. The Coast Path starts from the seafront near number 15, the thatched cottage at 1.

14km (9 miles) or two walks of 7km (4 miles) and 8km (5 miles).
The scenery is very good. With exceptional coastal and inland views.
Usually good walking all year.
Some steep slopes.
Overall from sea level up to 284m.
Minehead is on a regular bus route.
There is a car park on the seafront at Minehead at 1.
There are tearooms and pubs in Minehead.

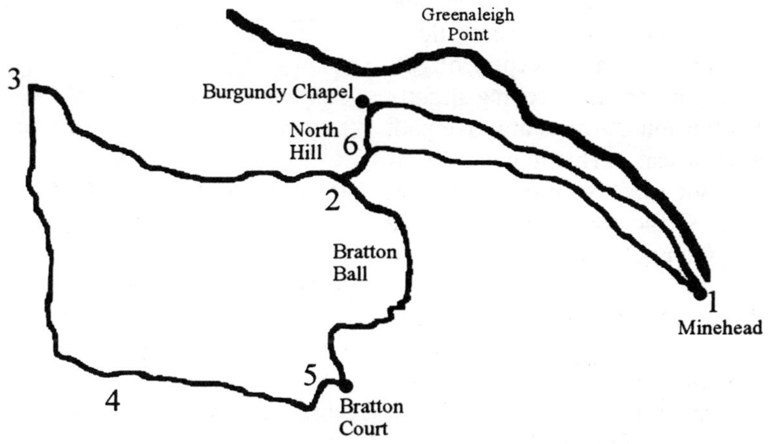

1.(971470) There are a couple of signs pointing to the start of the South West Coast Path and our route follows the Coast Path up beside the thatched cottage towards the next street, before which it turns off to the right. After about 2km, at the top of the hill and just after a very sharp left bend in the path, there is a five path junction at 2

2.(947477) Here the Coast Path turns right. For the next 2km the Coast Path is fairly obvious to where it crosses a tarmac track at 3.

3.(925483) Here our route leaves the Coast Path and turns left to follow that track to a lane and almost directly across that lane is a track. Our route follows that track around the top of a valley that is on the right, and then goes through a field gate. About 800m down that track from the gate our route meets a tarmac lane and turns left on it to reach a stile after about 450m and where the lane bends abruptly right at 4.

4.(932464) Over this stile our route goes along the edge of the plantation and then out into a field where our route continues for about 300m across the field with a holly hedge to the left until there is a gate to the left from where a path, with a field hedge to the right, runs down the side of the field to a lane. Our route turns right on that lane for about 100m and then turns left down a track that is opposite the farm buildings at Bratton Court to go into the wood at 5.

5.(945468) In the wood our route keeps to the right for about 150m and then follows the zigzag up through the wood until there is a stile on the right. Over the stile our route continues to a tarmac lane on which it turns right and then follows the next track to the left. Keeping on that track for about 50m and keeping slightly to the left our route arrives at a five path junction by a seat. (This is point 2) At the five path junction our route goes straight across and down towards the sea for over 100m until just past a sharp right bend at 6.

6.(948479) Here there is a very steep small path to the left that goes down to the remains of Burgundy Chapel. Following this path down until there is a seat on the left, just before the path begins to rise, our route then turns right. It is quite easy to miss the chapel which is some way down that steep path. Where the path divides, just before the wood, there are some steps down to the chapel on the left. Returning up the steps from the chapel our route then continues, left, down through the woods. The path is fairly obvious all the way to Greenaleigh Farm. Following the track through the farm and on for about 500m our route then forks left on to a slightly narrower track. Just after where there are some railings around the head of a cleft in the cliff a smaller path forks to the left. Our route follows this path down towards the beach, through a car park, past the lifeboat station on the left and continues along the seafront and back to 1.

SHORT ROUTES.

Burgundy Chapel Part. 7km. our route follows the Coast Path from Minehead to 2 and then descends back down the same path for about 100m to follow the notes from 6.

North Hill and Bratton Ball Part. 8km. Following the notes from 2 our route returns to the same point.

Exmoor offers some of the most rugged cliff and coastal scenery in the country.

It is this ruggedness that has allowed much of the area to continue to be reasonably undeveloped and, fortunately, in more recent times the acquisition of much of the coast and inland valleys by conservation organisations should enable the present scene to remain unchanged for many years to come.

The walks between Minehead and Bossington are mild and scenically contrasting with not only the contrast of the coast and the hamlets in the inland wooded valleys but the seasonal contrast from spring when the clifftops are covered in thrift, through autumn when the heathers and late flowering western gorse cover the hill to those clear winter days when the view is forever and the snow can be clearly seen on the Brecon Beacons.

Bossington, Selworthy and Selworthy Beacon.

From the A39, Minehead to Porlock, turn right about 7km (5 miles) on to a minor road through Allerford to Bossington. There is a car park in Bossington at 1.

8km (5 miles).
The scenery is the very best. With exceptional coastal and inland views over farmland and moorland.
Usually good walking all year.
Some steep slopes.
Overall from about 15m up to 308m.
Bossington is on a regular bus route.
There is a car park in Bossington at 1.
There are tearooms in Bossington and tearooms and pubs in Porlock.

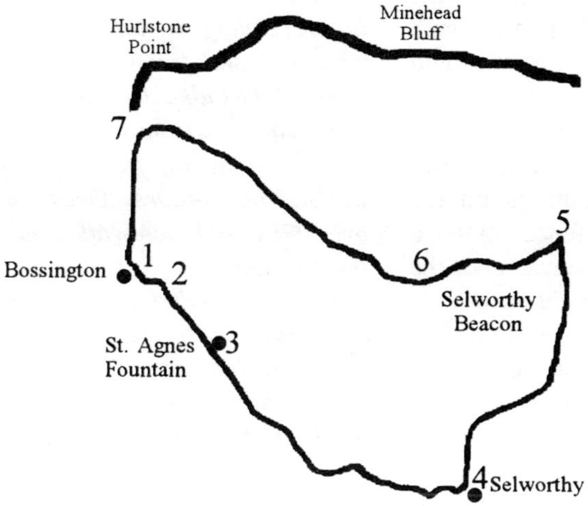

1.(898480) From the car park near the river at Bossington, at 1, our route goes over the river on the footbridge and turns right, then right again through a small gate to follow a path that climbs the bank above the river. From here the path is fairly obvious to a large manor house, now holiday flats, at West Lynch at 2.
2.(902478) Here the path forks and our route takes the left fork to continue above the house and then directly on, past another broad path that forks down to the right after the house.
3.(904474) St. Agnes Fountain is where six paths meet and there is a clearing on the right offering good views over Porlock Bay and to the left a small waterfall runs over some stones. From here our route continues in the same direction, past the fountain and keeping to the left. Many paths cross or join our route which continues to Selworthy where there are some thatched cottages 50m or so to the right. Here our route keeps to the right at a fork in the paths to come to a stile. Turning left over this stile and then crossing the brook on the stone slab to come to another stile. Over this stile our route turns right to go up to and join a track at 4. (The village on the right is Selworthy).
4.(919469) Turning left on the track our

route goes through the woods with the brook down on the left for about 1km. Our route then goes across the upper part of the brook where the track leaves the woodland and continues up the hill until almost near the top where a broad track crosses our route. Turning left on to it and then taking the right fork when the path divides our route reaches a lane. Almost directly across this lane is a tarmac track that runs across the moorland. Our route follows this track until it joins a track by the edge of a field fence at 5.

5.(925483) This track is the Coast Path and our route turns left on to it and after about 200m the Coast Path is on the moorland side of a field fence. After a further 500m the field fence and the Coast Path turn abruptly right at 6.

6.(916480) Selworthy Beacon is not on the Coast Path and the view from it can be seen by turning left for about 200m at 6. From 6 onwards the Coast Path is not always obvious because it goes across open land with a number of paths worn on it. As the Coast Path progresses towards Bossington there is a hill with a stone cairn on it, ahead and slightly to the left. That hill slopes down to the right and then drops to a steep sided combe called Hurlstone Combe. It is down that combe that the Coast Path goes until it reaches a field fence where it turns left. However, at that point it is possible to turn right to the old coastguard building at Hurlstone Point, at 7, to enjoy the views across Porlock Bay and beyond before returning to follow the Coast Path to the footbridge and the car park at 1.

Beyond Porlock the scenery is more rugged and includes some of the highest cliffs in the country where less common sea birds breed in summer and where, inland, fast flowing rivers fall through deep valleys.

The stunted oaks on the cliffs, with their flattened, wind pruned outline, are the same species that are growing broad and tall in the valleys that cut deep into the moors.

In preceeding centuries the moorlands were wet and frequently impassable so many of the bulky items were delivered by sea, frequently from south Wales, with the boat standing off from the rocky coves whilst the sailors threw the goods overboard and men waded out to collect the consignment.

Lime was needed to improve the acid moorland soil for farming and there are many derelict lime kilns along the north Devon coast from where the lime could be taken inland in small quantities.

In many places the solid rock cliffs provided the only dry base for tracks and these were developed to make the first coast roads which today remain in many places as minor coast roads or tracks that are frequently on, or very near, the clifftop.

There are still many places where the moorland comes down to the sea although there have been attempts to farm this part of Exmoor. There were some grandiose schemes in the last century that included a private railway to the coast for fertilisers and other supplies to be carried inland and for produce to be taken out.

There was also a grandiose scheme for a resort at Woody Bay and the base of the pier can be seen at low tide.

Porlock, Bossington, Porlock Bay and Porlock Weir.

8km (5 miles).
The scenery is good.
Usually good walking all year.
Almost level.
Overall from about sea level up to 60m.
Porlock is on a regular bus route.
There are car parks in Porlock.
There are tearooms and pubs in Porlock and a tearoom and a pub at Porlock Weir.

Porlock is on the A39, 9km (6 miles) west of Minehead.

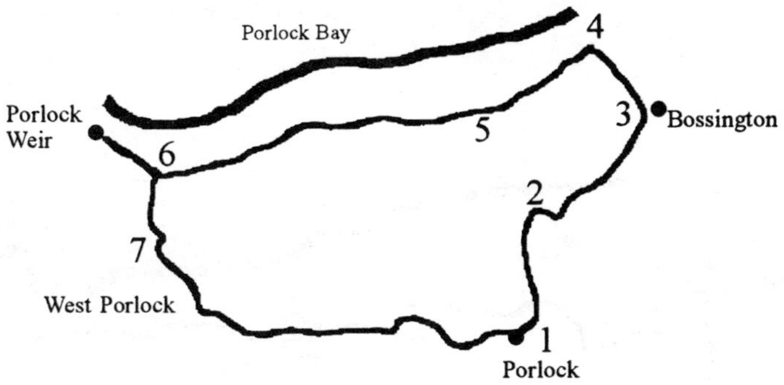

1.(889469) Villes Lane turns off north from the main street in Porlock about 250m to the east of the church. At the far end of Villes Lane a path continues directly on to 2 where it forks for either Porlock Bay or Bossington.

2.(889475) Our route ignores the stile and bends right to Bossington where it joins a track at a farmstead at 3.

3.(896480) At Bossington our route turns left on the track around the farmstead and then turns left on another track, which is the Coast Path, to Porlock Bay at 4.

4.(893484) At Porlock Bay the Coast Path continues left and is on the field side of the field fence for about one kilometre where it goes through a small gate at 5 and continues westwards to Porlock Weir, remaining on the field side of the pebble ridge.

6.(867477) At Porlock Weir there is a concrete sea wall on the left and about 50m along this wall the path goes up some steps to the road where the Coast Path turns right and our route turns left, back towards Porlock. About 500m along the road towards Porlock a small path turns off to the right at 7.

7.(867473) Our route goes up that path and arrives at what looks like a disused village hall. Our route follows the path near the left side of the building to veer left over a footbridge. From here back to Porlock our route goes along the edge of the wood to join a tarmac road on which our route turns left, into Porlock.

Porlock Weir, Culbone, and Robber's Bridge.

From the A39, Minehead to Lynton, turn off right in Porlock on to the B3225 to Porlock Weir.

16km (10 miles) or two walks both of 8km (5 miles).
The scenery is outstanding. The Coast Path is slightly inland, above and away from the cliff edge, and the inland route is mainly over moorland and through woodland.
Usually good walking all year.
Some steep slopes.
Overall from sea level up to 405m.
Porlock Weir is on a regular bus route.
There is a car park at Porlock Weir.
There is a tearoom and a pub at Porlock Weir and a pub between 6 and 7 on the walk.

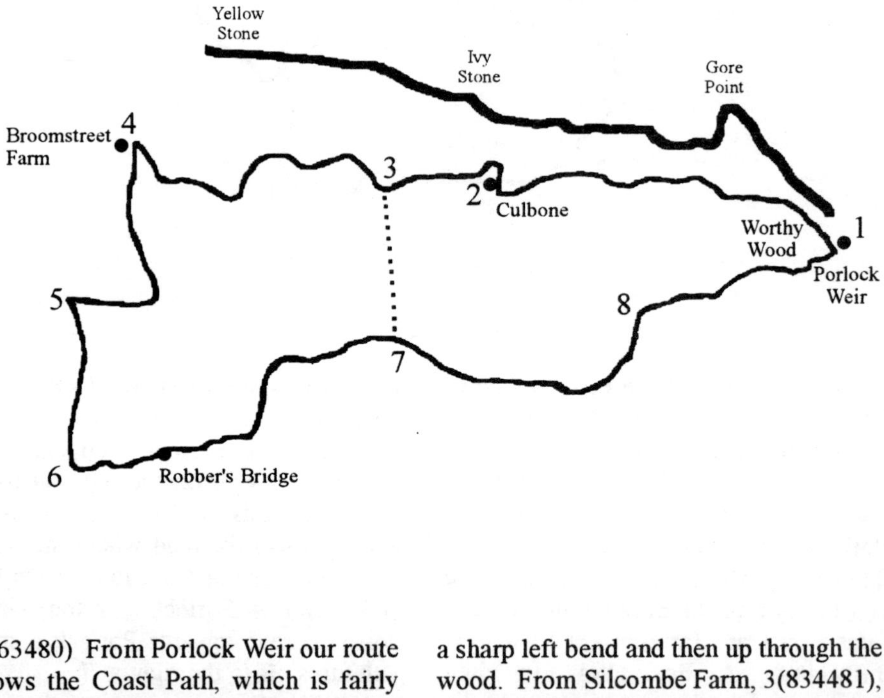

1.(863480) From Porlock Weir our route follows the Coast Path, which is fairly well signed, from the back of the pub and then through the fields to a lane on which it turns right. At the toll gate the Coast Path passes to the cliff side of the toll house and from there on is fairly obvious to Culbone Church at 2.

2.(842482) Leaving Culbone by the track that has Culbone Church on the right the Coast Path continues up the track, around a sharp left bend and then up through the wood. From Silcombe Farm, 3(834481), the Coast Path continues along the track for about 2km until just before Broomstreet Farm. When the roof of the farm can just be seen from the Coast Path there is a tarmac lane to the left at 4.

4.(817484) Our route leaves the Coast Path and follows that lane up to the A39. Directly across the A39 is a track and our route goes across the A39 to a stile, which is to the right of the track, and over the stile continues on the field side of the fence along the right hand side of the track. After about 50m, in the corner of the field, our route turns right keeping to the right of the hedge bank. When that hedge bank turns abruptly away to the left our route goes over the stile and continues on along the track across the moorland for about 300m to a junction of four paths at the corner of a plantation.

5.(814474) Our route turns left at this crossing and remains on that moorland path until near the corner of some fields on the right. There is a broad path that runs down the moorland side of the field but our route takes the narrow path to the left of it to pass to the right of an ancient disused field bank with trees growing on it before coming to a field gate. Our route goes through that gate and then down the steep slope to cross a footbridge on to a tarmac lane.

6.(814464) Turning left on the lane our route goes up the hill to a bridge over a river. This is Robber's Bridge and where the tarmac lane bends to the right our route continues straight on to a small gate. Through the gate our route climbs the hillside to the right and then follows a track to the Culbone Inn. Our route goes to the right of the Culbone Inn and then goes across the A39 on to a tarmac road. About 500m along that road a track turns off to the right at 7.

7.(835472) Our route follows that track as it gradually descends to the brook which it does cross at a small ford and then our route takes the left track to continue down the right side of the brook. Turning left before the buildings at the first farmstead, Pitt Farm, our route continues down the farm drive and then down a lane with a brook to the right for about 300m to a bridge on the right at **8**.

8.(852472) Our route goes over the bridge and follows the track up the hill and near the edge of the wood for about 600m and then follows a small path off to the left that meanders down through the wood. Continuing down and across a track until about 700m down from the top of the wood, our route goes around the head of a shallow combe to take a small path down to the left that doubles back on the track and is very easy to miss. It is before the tarmac lane at the hairpin bend. Down that small path and through the dip in the combe our route continues to the tarmac lane at Porlock Weir. On the tarmac our route turns right and then left to return to the pub.

SHORT ROUTES.

Culbone Part. 8km. Following the notes through from 1, Silcombe Farm at 3 is the first farm after the woods that surround Culbone Church. About 100m before this farm is a track to the left that goes up through a field and here our route leaves the Coast Path to go up this track, with a field hedge on the right, and then continues on a more obvious track from the top of the field. Our route continues on that track to a tarmac road, turns left on it and, at 7, takes the first track on the right that gradually goes down into the combe and from there on follows the notes.

Robber's Bridge Part. 8km. This begins on the tarmac road that leads off the A39 opposite the Culbone Inn. About 350m along that road there is a track off to the left near 7. Turning left down that track and continuing on down to 3, at the bottom of the field, our route then turns left on the Coast Path through Silcombe Farm and then follows the notes back to the Culbone Inn.

Black Gate, Malmsmead and Old Barrow Hill.

On the A39 between Porlock and Lynton the Somerset and Devon County boundary is marked near an Exmoor Park visitor centre. Travelling on towards Lynton for about 1km there is a parking area on the left at Black Gate, at 1, just before a cattle grid.

12km (8 miles) or two walks of 7km (4 miles) and 8km (5 miles).
The scenery is outstanding. The Coast Path is mainly above the cliffs through farmland, and the inland route is through heath, moorland and a river valley.
Usually good walking all year but if there has been continuous heavy rain and the river is over the banks at 2 it is probably best to turn back and try again another day.
Some steep slopes.
Overall from 229m up to 393m.
There is a seasonal bus service along the A39 between Lynton and Porlock and this passes County Gate, Black Gate at 1 and Lillycombe at 4.
There are car parks at 1, at County Gate and at Malmsmead.
There is a tearoom and a pub at Brendon.

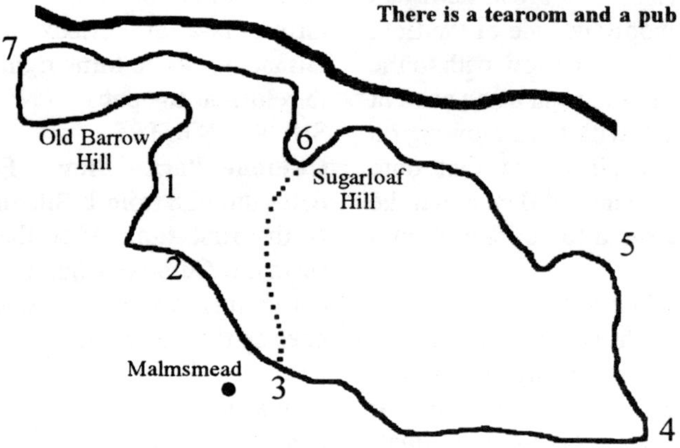

1.(788488) From the car park our route follows a path southwards, down over the moorland. The path starts about 20 metres out from the field boundary and draws progressively nearer to the fields on the right as it goes down for about 600m, passing the first path on the left, to then follow the next obvious path to the left that can be seen to go down to the river at 2.

2.(789486) From here our route continues upstream for about 1km to just beyond the second footbridge. (To get to Malmsmead, which is about 300m off our route, it is necessary to cross the river here and then turn right on the tarmac lane.) Continuing upstream our route turns left between two field banks and then right through the first field gate at 3.

3.(795480) From here our route continues in the same direction, past Oaremead Farm on the right, along the edge of the fields for about 500m to then turn right on a lane and then left into a riverside field at the gate before the bridge. About 100m upstream from the gate a very obvious ridge begins on the left and our route goes up that ridge. At the top of the ridge our route is on the edge of the moorland with the field edge to the right. Our route continues to rise slightly to where the combe on the left levels out and then continues straight on whilst the field boundary bears away to the right. At the top of the slight rise four paths meet at the corner of a plantation and from here our route continues directly on to a stile. Over the stile our route continues along a track with a field bank to the right, and on to a field gate. Our route remains in the same field and turns left up to a stile on the right that leads on to the road at 4.

4.(819475) Directly across the main road there is a lane and our route continues to the bottom of the lane to join the Coast Path and turns left through Broomstreet Farm at 5.

5.(817484) From Broomstreet Farm the Coast Path is fairly obvious for about 3km to where it is quite easy to miss the small turning off the track where the Coast Path turns off the track and goes past Sisters Fountain at 6.

6.(793491) There is a small path that goes down some steps to the right and about ten metres from the track the Coast Path passes an ancient cross by a spring, this is Sisters Fountain. Then the Coast Path continues up to join a track on which it turns right for about 300m to a small path off to the left. That small path is the continuation of the Coast Path which is fairly obvious for the next 1.5km where it very noticeably turns inland at Wingates Combe to 7.

7.(780496) Where the Coast Path goes across the brook that flows down through the combe our route turns off left to follow a path up through the combe and then to the left to come out from the trees at a small gate where it continues up a field, with a field bank to the right, to a plantation. Our route goes over a stile and up through the plantation to another field. Our route turns left in the field to continue around the top edge of the plantation and then turns right on a track. In the field to the right of the track there is the earthwork remains of a Roman fort on Old Barrow Hill. The track does pass a stile on the right from where it is possible to walk to the earthworks. Our route continues along that track to the A39 and a few hundred metres to the right is the car park at 1.

SHORT ROUTES.

Old Barrow Hill Part. 7km. Following the notes through to the footbridge just before 3 this route continues upstream for a few metres to then turn left between two field banks. After about 50m this route continues towards the left and up to the top of the steepest part of the slope and then on to the car park at County Gate. Turning left on the road for about 50m this route then turns off right down a track. At the bottom this route turns right on another track for a few metres to join the Coast Path at 6 where there are some steps down to the left to where the Coast Path goes past a stone cross by Sisters Fountain and from where the notes can be followed back to Black Gate.

Sugarloaf Hill Part. 8km. From the car park on the A39 at County Gate there is a path going south, to the right of the main road to Minehead, and this path does go down to the river near 3. Following the notes from 3 to 6, where the Coast Path turns off right at Sisters Fountain, here our route leaves the Coast Path and carries on along the track for a few metres to go up the next track on the left to the A39 about 50m from the car park at County Gate.

Countisbury, Watersmeet, Brendon and Kipscombe.

About 2km from Lynmouth on the A39 to Minehead there is a car park on the left, at 1, opposite the pub called the Exmoor Sandpiper.

12km (8 miles).
The scenery is the very best. Much of the inland part is through the wooded valley of the East Lyn River.
Usually good walking all year.
Overall from 110m up to 332m.
There is a seasonal bus service between Lynton and Minehead and this passes the Exmoor Sandpiper, at 1, and Wingate Farm, at 4.
There is a car park at 1 and parking is possible at 3, at Brendon.
There are tearooms at Brendon and pubs at Countisbury, Rockford and Brendon.

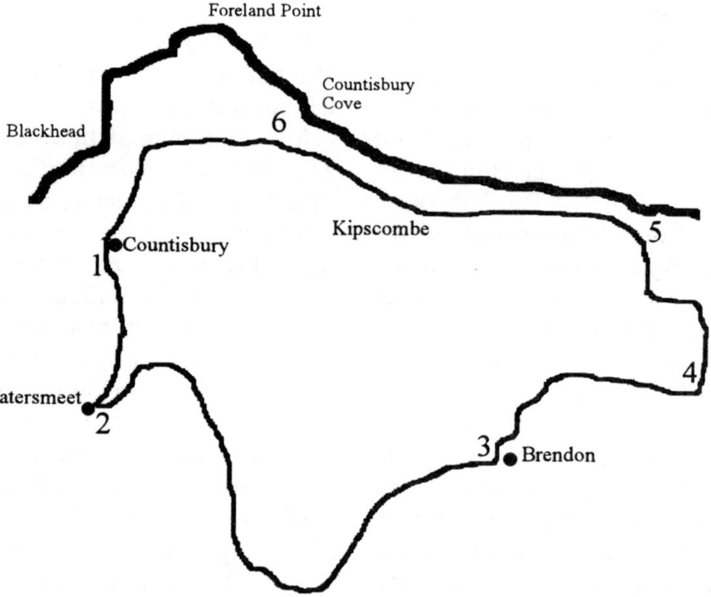

1.(747497) Leaving the car park our route turns left up the A39 for about 50m to go through the first gate on the right. When the track enters a field our route continues near the left side of the field but gradually moves away from the left side so that when the gorse on the far side is reached our route is about 80m from the left field bank and goes down through the gorse to a gate. Through the gate our route continues along the ridge and then winds its way down through the trees to the river at 2.

2.(745486) Our route turns right and then goes across the river on the first footbridge, turns left up the right bank of the river to cross back over the river at the next footbridge and then continues upstream on the left bank of the river for about 4km to Brendon at 3.

3.(768483) At Brendon our route turns right on to a lane. Passing a packhorse bridge and then a road bridge on the right our route continues up a lane that climbs gradually to the A39 where our route turns right on to a path between the road and the fields for about 500m to 4.

4.(782489) Past the entrance to Wingate Farm, which is on the opposite side of the road, there is a gate on the left side of the road through which our path proceeds along a track with hedge banks on either side and then continues around the left side of the field to a plantation. Our route goes down through the left side of the plantation to a stile and continues down the left side of the field to a small gate. Through the gate our route continues down through the combe to join another path on which our route turns left at 5.

5.(785494) That path is the Coast Path and is fairly obvious for about 3km to where it joins a tarmac track that zigzags down the hillside on the left. Following the tarmac for about 100m the Coast Path then turns left on a path that goes up the side of the hill at 6. (However, many people find the view from near Foreland Point to be worth the few hundred metres extra walking and to gain that view it is necessary to leave the Coast Path and keep on the tarmac lane towards the lighthouse.)

6.(756504) Our route follows the Coast Path up the hill and when it reaches the cliff it keeps to the left and then goes along the cliff side. About 50m before Countisbury Church our route leaves the Coast Path to go over a stile into the right side of the churchyard. Going around the right side of the church and down the path on to a lane our route then turns right to the car park opposite the Exmoor Sandpiper.

Generally, the cliffs of north Exmoor have rounded tops and then a steep cliff. About 125,000 years ago the cliffs would have been more vertical but during a cold glacial period about 18,000 years ago the Bristol Channel became a dry plain. Then extreme weather conditions turned the steep cliffs into the gentle sloping cliffs the remains of which are the rounded cliff tops which have since been worn into steep cliffs as the seas returned.

One of the interesting parts of the scene in the walk beyond Lynmouth is the way that boulders lie about the Valley of Rocks. During the last ice age boulders broken away from the valley side would slide downwards quite fast in summer when the surface layer thawed but when the ice age ended and the top layer dried out they stopped moving.

Most of the steep sided valleys that run down to the coast had been formed by about 125,000 years ago and continued to deepen as glacial melt waters flooded through them.

The hills tend to be a little older than the valleys. Most of the hills were formed about 300 million years ago when land mass pressures buckled the area.

Not a lot has changed recently though and to quote a recent traveller "..the original rugged and picturesque surface of a great portion of the Valley of Rocks has not been disturbed."

Thomas Cooper, c.1853.

Lynmouth, Watersmeet and Countisbury.

The A39 from Minehead goes over the River Lyn in Lynmouth and turns off to the left immediately after the road bridge. Here there is a car park on the left at 1.

8km. (5 miles).
The scenery is the very best. The coastal views are good and most of the inland part is through a wooded river valley.
Usually good walking all year.
Some steep slopes.
Overall from 10m up to 290m.
Lynmouth is on a regular bus route.
There are car parks in Lynmouth and at Countisbury on the A39 opposite the Exmoor Sandpiper.
There are tearooms at Lynmouth and pubs at Lynmouth and Countisbury.

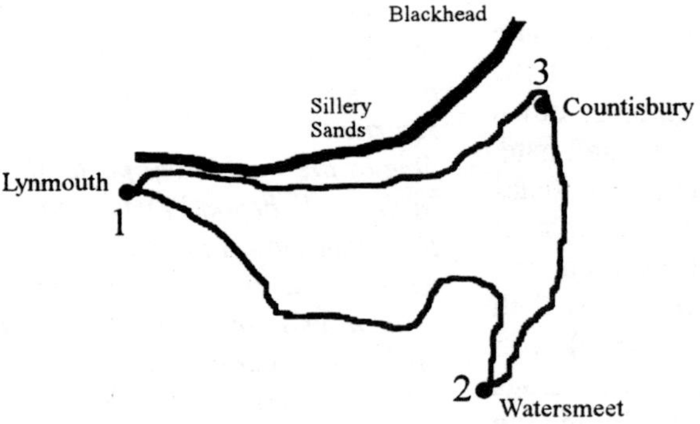

1.(725495) From the car park our route goes across the river on the road bridge of the A39 and continues upstream on a lane that follows the left bank of the East Lyn River. Where the lane ends our route continues upstream on a path that goes up through the river valley, remaining near the left bank, for a further 2.5km to where two rivers join at Watersmeet at 2.

2.(745486) At Watersmeet our route goes past the tearooms on the left and along the same riverside path for about 100m to the first path up through the woods on the left to continue along a modest ridge and then through a gate into a field. At the top right hand corner of the field our route joins a track which ends on the road. Turning left on the road for a few metres our route then follows the first lane on the right into Countisbury Churchyard and then follows the path around the left side of the church, over the stile and out of Countisbury Churchyard at 3.

3.(747498) Our route continues directly on for about 50m to turn left on the Coast Path on the cliff top. From Countisbury the Coast Path is above the cliff but then has to follow the road for about 250m before turning off right, down towards the beach, and then going across the East Lyn on a footbridge to turn left, back to 1.

Lynton, Valley of Rocks and Woody Bay.

Approaching Lynton from Lynmouth on the B3234 take the first turning on the right that is signed into Lynton. The first public car park on the left is at 1.

13km (8 miles) or two walks of 8km (5 miles) and 5km (3 miles).
The scenery is the very best.
Usually good walking all year.
Some steep slopes.
Overall from 15m up to 271m.
Lynton is on a regular bus route.
There are car parks at Lynton, The Valley of Rocks, Lee Bay and above Woody Bay.
There are tearooms at Lynton and Lee and there are pubs at Woody Bay and Lynton.

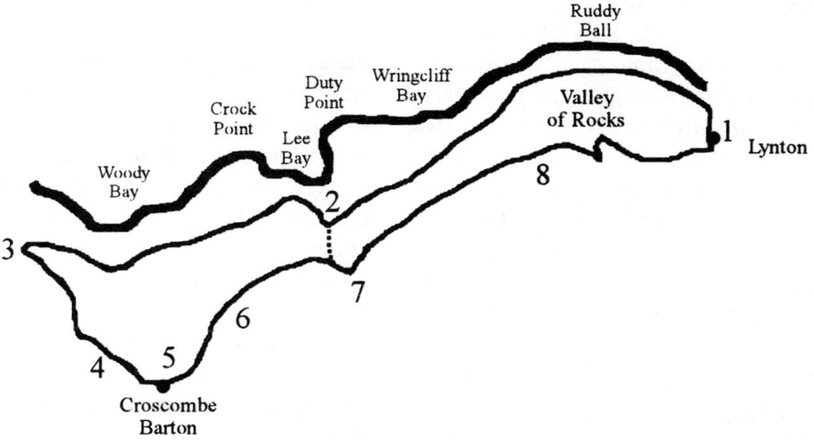

1.(721494) Our route follows the road into Lynton and takes the first path on the right, just past the church to continue on to the Coast Path which is fairly obvious through to Lee Bay and on to Woody Bay. Just before Woody Bay the Coast Path turns off the lane from Lee Abbey, right, down on to a path through the woods to join a track at 3.

3.(676488) On this track the Coast Path turns left but many people find the .5km walk down the track to the right, to the sea at Woody Bay to be worthwhile. Our route follows the Coast Path left on the track to a sharp left bend where the Coast Path turns off right. Our route leaves the Coast Path here and continues up the track to a lane. Directly across that lane is a track up through the wood and our route follows that track to another lane. Turning left our route continues around the sharp left bend for about a further

100m to then turn right up a track, just before the farm called Slattenslade. About 50m up that track our route turns left over a stile at 4.

4.(678483) Our route goes directly up through the fields, keeping to the right of the field bank all the way for about 300m to where there is a stile on the left. Over that stile our route continues in approximately the same direction for just over 200m to where a footpath is signed down to the buildings at Croscombe Barton, which can be seen down in the valley, and an alternative route is signposted over a stile to the left. Our route goes over the stile to follow the alternative route and continues directly across the field to a gate through which our path turns right on a track down to the farm, but, our route turns left off the track, over a stile and down some steps into the field, before the buildings, at 5.

5.(684480) Running through that field is a brook and if this area should be particularly muddy there is always the footpath that is on the dry track nearer the house. Our route goes up the steps and stile on the opposite side of the field and turns left to go down the track for about 400m to continue to the right of the brook when the track goes over a bridge at 6.

6.(686483) Our turning off to the right is along a small path that winds its way through the wood to eventually meet a track at a very sharp bend. Our route turns left, on to the track, and continues on that track for about 1km to where, about 200m after the track has crossed a concrete bridge at 7(696487), the track forks. Our route takes the right fork and continues up for about 600m to the moorland at 8.

8.(701492) There are many minor paths over the moorland. Our route climbs progressively up and to the right, almost to the top of the moorland. Before the edge of the moorland our route bears to the left to meet a field bank which remains to the right of our route as it climbs to the top of the brow. Continuing on down, now close to the field bank on the right, until the cemetery can be seen down on the left our route turns left at the next junction. Our route continues on that path until turning off, right, across the field by the side of the cemetery and on to the road where our route turns right through the centre of Lynton, to 1.

SHORT ROUTES.

Valley of Rocks Part. 8km. Following the Coast Path through from 1, past Lee Abbey to the first small toll cottage on the left this short route leaves the Coast Path here to go up the path by the side of the cottage on the left. Continuing up and to the right, through the wood, for about 400m this path joins a track on which it turns left to a concrete bridge at 7 from where it follows the main notes.

Woody Bay Part. 5km. From the car park at Lee, which is opposite the toll cottage at 2(695490), this route turns right on the tarmac lane and follows the Coast Path and the main notes through to 6 where the path meets a track at a sharp bend at 6. Following the notes from 6 it becomes possible to see a brook down on the left. Our route soon leaves the track to follow a small path that goes off to the left and then remains near the right bank of the brook down to the car park opposite the toll cottage.

Hunter's Inn, Trentishoe Down, Kittitoe and Slattenslade.

Turn left off the A39, Blackmoor Gate to Lynmouth, at Martinhoe Cross on to a minor road signed to Woody Bay. Follow the signs to Woody Bay for about 2km from the A39 and turn right past a car park on the right. After a left bend and a very steep right bend there is a car park on the right at 1.

17km (11 miles) or two walks of 7km (4 miles) and 11km (7 miles).
The scenery is the very best. An unusually good contrast of scenic coast, moorland and wooded river valleys.
Usually good walking all year.
Some steep slopes.
Overall from 40m up to 295m.
There are no bus services to this walk.
There are car parks at 1, near 2 and near 7.
There are tearooms at Lynton and Combe Martin. There are pubs at Woody Bay, about 500m east of 1, and Hunter's Inn.

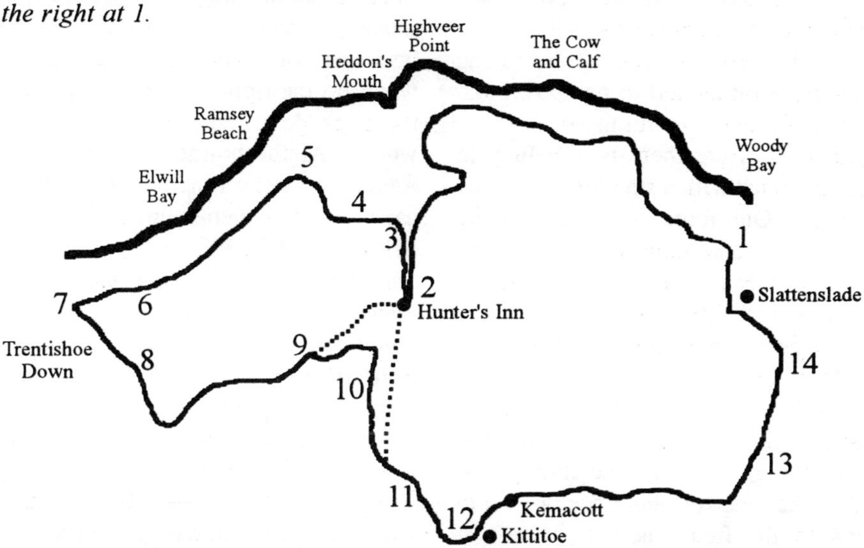

1.(676486) Depending on which map is preferred the Coast Path takes either of two routes between Woody Bay and Hunter's Inn. From here our route follows the Coast Path up the coast road to a very sharp left bend where it turns off to the right along a broad track to just before The Hunter's Inn at 2.

2.(655482) Just before the Hunter's Inn a path turns off to the right to go back downstream on the right bank and our route follows this path to cross the stream on the Coast Path near 3(655488) and to then continue about half way up the zigzag on the opposite side to 4.

4.(652489). About half way up the zigzag there is a choice of paths. Either right along a narrow decaying path which some maps show as the Coast Path and which rejoins at 5(649491) or up the zigzag to turn right at the top and to continue with the wall on the left to pass 5 and to continue to 6.

6.(635483). Here the Coast Path goes into a field for about 300m and then comes out on to the moorland at 7.

7.(632482) Our route leaves the Coast Path a few metres after it leaves the field to come out on to the moorland and then turns left up the moorland side of the fields to a junction of three tarmac lanes. Our route follows the middle lane down the hill for about 100m to then turn off to the right at 8.

8.(636479) Here our route goes down the dip in the bracken covered side of Trentishoe Down. At the bottom our route turns left on the tarmac track for about 30m and then veers off right along a path for about 1km to where it goes over the river on a footbridge. A few metres up that track, past the buildings, there is a staggered crossing of tracks at 9.

9.(650479) Here our route follows the second track on the left to go up through the wood for about 600m to 10.

10.(653478) Here there is a field gate across the track with a smaller gate to the left of it. Our route goes through the smaller gate and continues for about 250m to go through a field gate on the left and down a track which has some large beech trees on an ancient stone bank on the left, to 11.

11.(656470) Here our route crosses the stream on the footbridge and continues through the gate over by the cottage and then up the lane for about 500m to turn off on to the first lane on the left at Kittitoe.

12.(661468) From the junction our route goes up this lane for about 500m to an abrupt bend to the left and continues around this bend, up and around a bend to the right and then down a lane to Kemacott. In the farmyard our route follows a track to the left, between some buildings, and up into a field. Keeping the banked hedge to the right for about 1200m until it turns abruptly away to the right our route continues directly on for about 90m to a field gate that leads on to a lane. Here our route turns left for about 200m to a stile on the right at 13.

13.(678471) Over the stile our route goes across the field and keeps to the left of what was a hedge and then goes across a lane by way of two stiles to continue in the same direction for about 750m to 14.

14.(681480) Ignoring the stile and then the field gate to the right our route bears to the left to remain in the same field, keeping the banked hedge to the right, to continue on through fields and gates to a stile on to a track. Turning right down the track for about 50m our route turns left on a lane just before Slattenslade. The lane bends to the right and then there is a wood on the right and our route follows the track down the nearest edge of the wood. At the bottom of the track our route turns left on the tarmac lane to the car park a few metres up the hill.

SHORT ROUTES.

Turn left off the A39, Blackmoor Gate to Lynmouth, just after Parracombe on to a minor road signed to Hunter's Inn.

Slattenslade Part. 11km. Looking towards the front of the Hunter's Inn Hotel our route goes down the lane to the left, through the field gate on the left from which a track leads up through the woods and then down to the footbridge near 11 from where this path follows the notes through to the end and then from 1 back to the Hunter's Inn.

Trentishoe Down Part. 7km.
Looking towards the front of the Hunter's Inn Hotel our route follows a track that goes along the right side of it, then follows a path that leads off it to the left and continues near the right bank of the stream to 3(655488) in the notes. From 3 our route follows the notes to 9. Here our route takes the first path on the left to continue on the right of the river to a lane on which our route turns right to the Hunter's Inn.

Combe Martin, Trentishoe Down and Great Hangman.

Combe Martin is on the A399 about 6km (4 miles) east of Ilfracombe.

17km (11 miles) or two walks of 6km (4 miles) and 12km (8 miles).
The scenery is outstanding and includes heath, a wooded river valley, farmland and exceptionally good coastal scenery.
Usually good walking all year.
Some modest slopes and a steep one near Trentishoe.
Overall from sea level up to 318m.
Combe Martin is on a regular bus route.
There are car parks in Combe Martin and on Trentishoe Down near 7.
There are tearooms and pubs at Combe Martin.

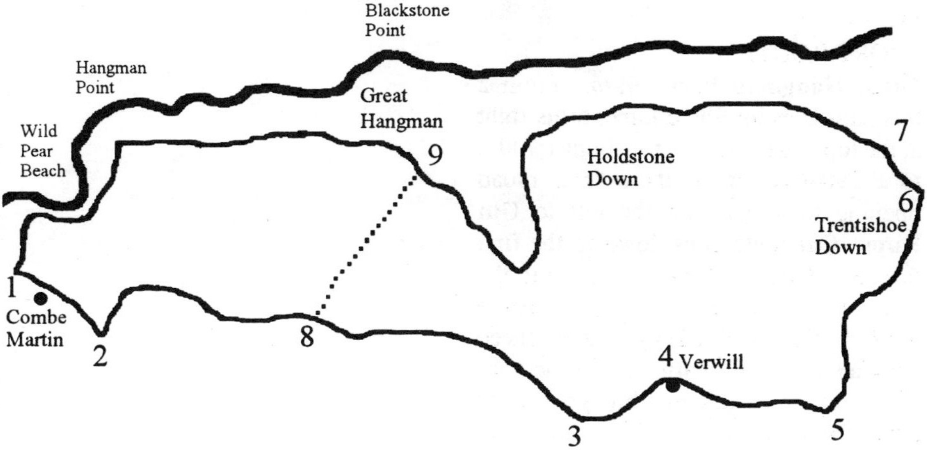

1.(577472) From the bay at Combe Martin our route goes about 1km up the main street to Shute Lane on the left at 2.
2.(583468) Our route goes up Shute Lane to turn right at the top and then continues along a lane for about 3km to a four lane crossroads at 3.
3.(615462) Our route turns left at the crossroads for about 100m to then turn right down a narrow tarmac lane to Verwill Farm at 4.
4.(622465) Through this farmstead our route turns right where the buildings end to follow a sunken lane that eventually comes out into a field. Our route continues across the fields on the remains of the old track that can be seen as it curves slightly to the left and then to the right before our route passes through a field gate and on to a lane on which it turns right for about 100m to a track that turns off on the left at 5.
5.(633462) From here our route goes down the track to a bridge over a brook that is just past the site of Trentishoe Mill and then rises gently before going down and around the grounds of Trentishoe Manor. Just past the entrance to Trentishoe Manor there is a smaller path called Ladies Mile Path that leads off to the left. Our route follows this for about 700m to just above the tree line and then turns left up a path that goes up through the dip in the bracken to a lane at 6.

6.(636479) On the lane our route turns left to a three lane junction and continues directly on to the moorland and then follows a path that approximately follows the outline of the fields on the right down towards the cliffs, meeting the Coast Path at 7 where it comes out from a corner of the field.

7.(632482) Our route turns left on the Coast Path which is fairly obvious as it continues over the moorland to Combe Martin.

SHORT ROUTES.

Great Hangman Part. 6km. From 2 this path goes up Shute Lane, turns right at the top and continues for about 1,700m to 8(598469) where there is a broad opening to a track on the left to Girt Farm. Our route goes down to the first farmhouse and continues, keeping to the right of the farmhouse and with a hedge bank to the right, through some sheep pens adjacent to a barn. From the barn our route continues on through a field gate from where the path is over moorland to 9(604478), which is about 800m from the farmhouse. At 9 the hedge bank turns abruptly away to the right and here our route turns left on the Coast Path which is fairly obvious to Great Hangman and back to Combe Martin.

Trentishoe Down Part. 12km. There is a car park near the edge of the moorland, at 7, near our route at Trentishoe Down. From here the notes indicate the way to the Coast Path on which our route turns left for about 2km to where a deep combe comes inland at Sherrycombe. About 600m after Sherrycombe the hedge bank on the left turns abruptly left and here our route leaves the Coast Path, at 9, to turn left and remain on the right of the hedge bank. Passing through a field gate and then through some sheep pens adjacent to a barn our route continues along a track to a farmhouse where the track veers to the left. Continuing along the track to a lane our route turns left on the lane to a four lane crossroads. This is 3 in the notes and from here the notes indicate the route back to 7.
